THE USBORNE
BOOK OF
FACTS
AND
RECORDS

Contents

AMAZING ANIMALS

Sarah Khan

Edited by Phillip Clarke

Designed by
Luke Sargent and Adam Constantine

Digital imagery by Keith Furnival

Consultant: Dr Margaret Rostron

Internet Links

Throughout this book, we have suggested interesting websites where you can find out more about the animal world. To visit the sites, go to the **Usborne Quicklinks website** at **www.usborne-quicklinks.com** and type the keywords "book of facts". There you will find links to click on to take you to all the sites. Here are some of the things you can do on the websites:

• Become a dolphin-trainer.

• Become a wildlife photographer.

• Find your way through a virtual rainforest.

• Make your own animal.

Site availability

The links in **Usborne Quicklinks** are regularly reviewed and updated, but occasionally you may get a message that a site is unavailable. This might be temporary, so try again later, or even the next day. If any of the sites close down, we will, if possible, replace them with suitable alternatives, so you will always find an up-to-date list of sites in **Usborne Quicklinks**.

Internet safety

When using the Internet, please make sure you follow these guidelines:

• Ask your parent's or guardian's permission before you connect to the Internet.

• If you write a message in a website guest book or on a website message board, do not include any personal information such as your full name, address or telephone number, and ask an adult before you give your email address.

• If a website asks you to log in or register by typing your name or email address, ask permission from an adult first.

• If you receive an email from someone you don't know, tell an adult and do not reply to the email.

• Never arrange to meet anyone you have talked to on the Internet.

Note for parents and guardians

The websites described in this book are regularly reviewed and the links in **Usborne Quicklinks** are updated. However, the content of a website may change at any time and Usborne Publishing is not responsible for the content on any website other than its own.

We recommend that children are supervised while on the Internet, that they do not use Internet Chat Rooms, and that you use Internet filtering software to block unsuitable material. Please ensure that your children read and follow the safety guidelines printed on the left. For more information, see the **Net Help** area on the **Usborne Quicklinks** website.

Computer not essential

If you don't have access to the Internet, don't worry. This book is complete on its own.

Amazing Animals Contents

Baby Animals

Many newborn animals are helpless and need a parent to feed and protect them. Mammals are the only animals that feed their babies with milk.

This mother pig can feed eight babies at once from teats on her body.

Animal	Name of young
Ape	Baby
Beaver	Kitten
Coyote	Whelp
Elephant	Calf
Goat	Kid
Gorilla	Infant
Hare	Leveret
Kangaroo	Joey
Llama	Cria
Platypus	Puggle

Water birth

Baby dolphins and whales can only stay underwater for about 30 seconds at a time. They need to swim up to the surface to breathe. As soon as a baby is born, its mother pushes it to the surface so it can take its first breath.

A baby whale is born tail first.

Its mother lifts it to the surface to breathe.

INTERNET LINK
For a link to a website where you can watch a slide show of baby animal photographs, go to **www.usborne-quicklinks.com**

Growth spurt

A newborn polar bear cub is only the size of a guinea pig. It will grow to be as big as a car.

This newborn polar bear is small enough to hide between its mother's toes.

At one year old, a polar bear cub is as big as a St. Bernard dog.

Pouch protection

A baby kangaroo is blind and so small that it could fit into a teaspoon. When a baby kangaroo is born, it crawls up into a pouch on its mother's stomach. It stays there for six months, until it is big enough to survive on its own.

A newborn kangaroo crawls from its mother's birth opening, up her tummy and into a pouch.

Inside the pouch, the baby fastens onto a teat to suck milk.

This baby kangaroo is getting too big for its mother's pouch. It is around six months old.

A female common vole can have babies when she is just 15 days old. She might have four to nine babies at a time, up to 15 times a year. In her lifetime, she may have 33 litters, giving birth to as many as 300 babies. This is more than any other mammal.

Some types of mouse opossum give birth to babies that are as small as grains of rice.

Holding on

A female opossum has 18 or so babies, and she keeps them all in one large pouch. After around ten weeks, the babies are too big for the pouch. Instead, they cling onto their mother's body anywhere they can – even onto her tail.

Mammals with longest pregnancies	Average pregnancy
African elephant	21 months
Asian elephant	20 months
White rhinoceros	16 months
Pilot whale	16 months
Camel	15 months
Black rhinoceros	15 months
Giraffe	14 months
Brazilian tapir	13 months
Blue whale	12 months
Sei whale	12 months
African buffalo	11 months
Walrus	11 months

Baby opossums cling onto their mother's body.

Growing Up

Although most newborn baby animals cannot look after themselves, some mature and become independent very quickly. Others need their mothers to look after them for a long time, protecting them from danger and teaching them how to find food.

Mean males

Young male hippos face an unusual danger in the form of older male hippos, who can be very fierce when guarding their territory. Young males stay near their mothers for protection.

Baby elephants are looked after by babysitters known as "aunties". When a mother elephant needs a break, another female from the herd looks after her baby. Sometimes aunties even produce milk to feed the baby. They will also care for the baby if the mother dies.

This male hippo is not yawning, but showing off his sharp teeth to warn off rivals.

Return to safety

A young kangaroo hides from danger in its mother's pouch.

Sensing danger, a young kangaroo runs to its mother's pouch.

It jumps in head first so that its tail and back feet are sticking out.

It then twists around inside the pouch and pokes its head out.

Growing up fast

Young gorillas develop twice as quickly as human babies. They begin to crawl at around two months old, ride on their mother's back at four months, and walk at nine months. They stay with their mothers until they are five years old.

This four-month-old gorilla is hitching a ride on its mother's back.

Animal	Age of maturity
Bushbaby	8 months
Bat	1-2 years
Kangaroo	2-3 years
Hyena	2-3 years
Lion	3-4 years
Giraffe	4-5 years
Rhinoceros	5-8 years
Hippopotamus	7-9 years
Gorilla	7-10 years
Chimpanzee	8-10 years
Elephant	10-13 years
Dolphin	10-16 years

INTERNET LINK
For a link to a website where you can play dolphin games, go to **www.usborne-quicklinks.com**

Dolphin friendships often last their whole lives.

Playtime

Young animals like to play, just like young children. Playing lets them practice hunting and survival skills. Young lions learn to fight and catch prey by pouncing on their playmates and swatting at their tails.

Young lions pretending to fight

Dolphin gang

A young dolphin stays with its mother for 3-6 years. When it leaves her, it joins a gang of other young dolphins. The gang stays together for years, spending most of the time playing together. They hardly ever mix with adults.

Dolphins play by balancing things on their snouts...

... blowing bubbles at each other...

! Shrews have big families, and they need to make sure no one gets lost. When the mother goes out for food, the children follow, each holding onto the one in front.

... and herding fish.

Life Goes On

Some animals live for only a matter of months, others live longer than humans. The length of time an animal lives is called its lifespan. The normal process of being born, growing up and breeding is called a life cycle.

Moles usually live for four years.

Mammals with shortest lives	Natural lifespan
1 Long-tailed shrew	12-18 months
2 Mole	3-4 years
3 Armadillo	4 years
4 European rabbit	up to 5 years
5 European hedgehog	6 years

Many animals die before completing their life cycle. They might:

• run out of food and starve

• be caught and eaten by a predator

• die of a deadly disease

Will this Arctic hare live to a ripe old age?

Sea life

Most sea animals, such as dolphins and whales, can live longer than most land animals. This may be because their bodies are cradled and supported by water and so are not worn out so quickly by the effects of gravity.

Dolphin

Scientists can work out the age of some dolphins and whales by looking inside their ears. They have plugs in their ears, made from layers of keratin (the substance which makes up hair and nails). Each year, new layers grow, a little like rings on a tree trunk. Scientists count the layers to tell how old the animal is.

Ear plug rings

Position of ear plug

INTERNET LINK
For a link to a website about the life cycle of elephants, go to
www.usborne-quicklinks.com

Mammals with longest lives	Natural lifespan
1 Bowhead whale	150-200 years
2 Fin whale	85-90 years
3 Human	75-80 years
4 Asian elephant	70-75 years
5 Orca	50-70 years

Long captivity

Animals in captivity usually live longer than animals in the wild because their life is easier and they have no predators.

Most shrews live fast and die young.

The oldest known orang-utan lived in Philadelphia Zoo, USA, and died at the age of 57. Orang-utans usually live for 40-45 years in the wild.

45　　57

The oldest known bat lived in London Zoo, England, and died at the age of 31. Bats usually live for 10-20 years in the wild.

20　31

The oldest known lion lived in Cologne Zoo, Germany, and died at the age of 29. Lions usually live for 12-14 years in the wild.

14　29

The oldest known tiger lived in Adelaide Zoo, Australia, and died at the age of 26. Tigers usually live for 10-15 years in the wild.

15　26

○ *Usual lifespan in the wild (years)*
● *Longest lifespan in captivity (years)*

Short life

Most shrews live for only 12-18 months in the wild. They are born one year, breed the next year and then die. The record lifespan for a shrew in captivity is two years and three months.

The oldest known elephant was a circus entertainer. During her career, Modoc, an Asian elephant, became a national heroine when she saved the circus lions from a terrible fire by dragging their cage out of a burning tent.

She starred in several American TV series before retiring to California, where she died in 1975, aged 75.

Modoc the Asian elephant had a long and glittering career.

Living room

Lemmings' lives follow strange four-year patterns. For three years, they breed and their population grows. In the fourth year, overcrowding makes them leave home in their millions, searching for more space. Their journey may be long and difficult, and many die on the way. Some even try to cross rivers and seas, drowning in the attempt.

Lemmings in search of more space

Animal Giants

Blue whales are the biggest animals that have ever lived. A female is around 30m long and can weigh as much as 190 tonnes – as heavy as 20 African elephants. Its tongue alone weighs three tonnes – heavier than 35 men. Its heart is as big as a car and its tail is as wide as the wings of an aeroplane.

A blue whale can dive to depths of 500m below the surface of the ocean.

Largest on land

Male African elephants are the largest animals on land. They weigh 4-7 tonnes and are around 3.5m tall at the shoulder – twice as tall as an average-sized person.

A male African elephant weighs as much as three family cars.

Kell, a Mastiff dog living in Leicestershire in England, is as heavy as a baby elephant. In 1999, the dog weighed 130kg. He is fed on a diet that contains lots of protein such as beef, eggs, and goat's milk.

Heavy jumper

Red kangaroos can grow up to 1.8m tall and weigh up to 90kg – as much as a heavyweight boxer. Their metre-long tails balance the weight of their bodies when they jump. They are the biggest of all pouched mammals, or marsupials.

Skyscrapers

With their long necks and legs, giraffes are the tallest animals. An adult Masai giraffe can be over 5m tall. A tall person only comes up to the top of its leg.

A Masai giraffe is three times as tall as this Masai warrior.

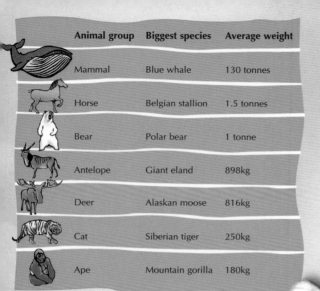

Animal group	Biggest species	Average weight
Mammal	Blue whale	130 tonnes
Horse	Belgian stallion	1.5 tonnes
Bear	Polar bear	1 tonne
Antelope	Giant eland	898kg
Deer	Alaskan moose	816kg
Cat	Siberian tiger	250kg
Ape	Mountain gorilla	180kg

Big appetite

Siberian tigers are the largest members of the cat family. They can grow to 3m from nose to tail and can weigh up to 300kg. They can eat as much as 45kg of meat in one night – enough to make 400 hamburgers.

A Siberian tiger can drag prey in its jaws that would be too heavy for six men.

INTERNET LINK

For a link to a website where you can find the biggest animals and other animal record-breakers, go to **www.usborne-quicklinks.com**

Brain box

Sperm whales have the heaviest brains. Their brains weigh up to 9kg – six times heavier than a human brain. The whale has a very large head which is around one third of its body length, so there is plenty of room for its huge brain.

Sperm whales are the world's largest meat-eating animals.

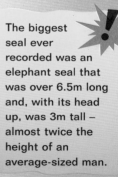

The biggest seal ever recorded was an elephant seal that was over 6.5m long and, with its head up, was 3m tall – almost twice the height of an average-sized man.

Small Animals

Savi's pygmy shrews are the world's smallest mammals. They are so small that they can look for food in tunnels made by earthworms.

Savi's pygmy shrew – the size of a finger.

The smallest dog ever known was a Yorkshire terrier the size of a hamster. It measured 6.3cm tall at the shoulder, only 9.5cm from nose to tail and it weighed just 113g.

Heartbeats

The smaller an animal is, the faster its heart beats. This is because smaller animals are more active than larger ones.

Animal	Average heart rate (beats per minute)
Horse	50
Cow	60
Human	70
Rabbit	200
Bat	300
Mouse	600
Shrew	800

INTERNET LINK
For a link to a website where you can visit a virtual small mammal house, go to **www.usborne-quicklinks.com**

The smallest horse in the world is Black Beauty, a miniature black mare the size of a cat. It is 47cm tall and weighs 19kg.

Animal group	Smallest species	Average weight (adult male)
Squirrel	African pygmy squirrel	10g
Monkey	Pygmy marmoset	120g
Rabbit	Pygmy rabbit	400g
Cat	Rusty-spotted cat	1.4kg
Fox	Fennec fox	1.5kg
Antelope	Royal antelope	1.5kg
Deer	Southern pudu	7kg
Bear	Sun bear	27kg
Dolphin	Commerson's dolphin	30kg
Seal	Ringed seal	60kg

Royal spoonful

Royal antelopes (the smallest antelopes in the world) have legs as thin as pencils. One living in London Zoo in England had hoofs so tiny that it was able to fit all four in a tablespoon.

Tiny tramplers

Southern pudus (the world's smallest deer) eat bamboo leaves, but are so small that they can only get to the leaves by first trampling on the bamboo stalks. This flattens the plant and brings the leaves within reach.

Southern pudu

Little record breakers

The silhouettes below show record-breaking animals at their actual size. They are shown in silhouette so you can easily compare their sizes.

Smallest marsupial
Long-tailed planigale:
9cm long,
weighs 4g

Smallest mammal
Savi's pygmy shrew:
6.5cm long,
weighs 2g

Smallest flying mammal
Bumblebee bat:
15cm wingspan,
weighs 1.9g

Smallest meat-eating mammal
Least weasel:
19cm long,
weighs 30g

What's For Dinner?

Animals need a lot of energy for hunting, finding homes and looking after their young. They get their energy from food.

Animal	How much it can eat in one day
Blue whale	5 tonnes of krill
Sperm whale	1 tonne of squid, fish and shrimp
African elephant	227kg of leaves
Polar bear	100kg of seal and fish
Hippopotamus	45kg of fruit and grass
Bengal tiger	45kg of red meat
Lion	36kg of red meat
Camel	32kg of fruit, leaves and grass
Giant panda	30kg of bamboo shoots
Bottlenose dolphin	15kg of fish
Brown bear	15kg of roots, leaves and red meat

Coming to get you... actually, vampire bats don't attack people.

Liquid diet

A great vampire bat drinks around 70% of its body weight in blood every night. Vampire bats attack sleeping animals. Their saliva contains a substance that stops the prey's blood from clotting and closing the wound while the bat feeds.

Low energy diet

A koala's diet doesn't give it much energy. It eats 600-800g of eucalyptus leaves each day. That is the same as a human surviving on just one bowl of cereal every day.

Koala

A Savi's pygmy shrew can't live for more than two hours without food and can eat up to three times its own weight in a day. A human would have to eat a sheep, 50 chickens, 60 loaves of bread and over 150 apples in one day to match the shrew's meals.

INTERNET LINK

For a link to a website where you can see whales catch their food, go to **www.usborne-quicklinks.com**

When a sea otter gets hungry in the water, it turns over onto its back, balances a large stone on its chest and opens clam shells by smashing them against the stone.

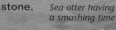

Sea otter having a smashing time

Scavenger hunt

Meat eaters don't always kill their own food. Sometimes they feed on animals that have been killed by other animals or have died naturally. This is called scavenging. Many predators, such as lions and wild dogs, often scavenge.

Blowing bubbles

Humpback whales sometimes make bubble "nets" to catch food.

The whale swims in an upward spiral, blowing air out of its blowhole to make bubbles.

The bubbles rise to the surface, forcing up the small fish and krill trapped within the spiral.

With its mouth open, the whale bursts out of the water and takes a huge gulp of food.

Gone fishing

Brown bears in Alaska, North America, fish for salmon that swim up mountain rivers to breed. They catch the fish in different ways.

They might snap up the fish in their powerful jaws...

...use their paws to flip the fish out of the water...

...or pin the fish to the river bed with their paws then grab them with their teeth.

A scavenging hyena has found part of a zebra for dinner.

How Animals Eat

Not many animals have hands, so they use other parts of their bodies to reach and grab their food.

Reaching up

Giraffes have the longest necks in the animal kingdom, measuring up to 1.8m. Because they have such long legs as well, they can reach leaves on the highest branches. They use their 50cm long tongues to grip and pull branches down. Then they strip off the leaves with their rubbery lips.

A giant anteater has a 60cm tongue. It tears open anthills and termite mounds with its claws and then pokes its long, sticky tongue inside, coating it with insects. It can flick its tongue in and out twice a second and can catch over 30,000 insects a day.

A giraffe's tongue is so tough that it can even grip thorns without getting hurt.

Terrific teeth

Animals have different types of teeth, depending on what food they eat.

Canines are dagger-like teeth that are used for piercing and killing prey.

Hyena

Canine

Carnassials are large, jagged teeth used for slicing meat.

Lioness

Carnassial

Incisors are small, front teeth that are used for biting and gnawing meat or plants.

Horse

Incisors

Molars are square teeth set inside an animal's cheek that are used for grinding plants.

Chimpanzee

Molars

Taking the strain

Instead of teeth, some whales have stiff fringes, called baleen, hanging down inside their mouths. They use the baleen like a strainer, to strain food from water. Baleen is made of keratin, a substance found in your fingernails and hair.

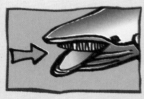

A whale opens its mouth and takes a huge gulp of water. The water is full of krill (small, shrimp-like creatures).

When it closes its mouth, the water is strained out through the baleen. The krill stays behind, trapped in the fringes.

Hyenas have such strong jaws and stomachs that they can chew up and digest the skin, bones, horns and even the teeth of their prey.

Strange stomachs

Cows have not one, but four stomach-like chambers in their bodies. After they have chewed and swallowed their food, it passes through two chambers, then comes back up to the mouth to be chewed again. Then it is swallowed for a second time and passes through the other two chambers. It is slowly digested along the way.

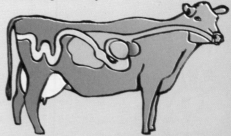

The four different colours show the four chambers inside a cow's body.

INTERNET LINK

For a link to a website about the different ways animals eat, go to **www.usborne-quicklinks.com**

Nosing around

Some animals use their noses not only to smell food, but to reach it as well.

African elephants use the two finger-like parts on the tips of their trunks to pick berries from the ground or pluck leaves from trees.

Echidnas poke their long, tough snouts into logs and termite mounds when searching for food.

Walruses drag themselves along the sea bed, using their muzzles to root out molluscs, worms and shrimps.

Noses can be used for grasping...

...poking...

...or digging.

Super Senses

Animals have five main senses:

 Touch

 Sight

 Hearing

 Smell

 Taste

Animals use their senses to collect information about their surroundings. Senses help them to find food, find a mate and avoid danger.

A bloodhound's nose is a million times more sensitive than a human's. It can follow a scent that is four days old.

Bloodhounds help the police to track down criminals by following their scent.

Ear for echoes

Bats and dolphins are the mammals with the most sensitive hearing. They can tell where objects are, and how big they are, by giving out high-pitched sounds. The sound waves bounce off the objects and return to the animal. This is called echo location.

A bat gives out a series of short, high-pitched sounds (shown in yellow).

The sounds bounce off nearby objects and return to the bat (returning sounds shown in blue).

Bright eyes

Cats are brilliant at seeing in the dark. They have a layer at the back of their eyes which acts like a mirror, reflecting and focusing light onto light sensor cells in their eyes.

In bright light, the dark hole, or pupil, in the cat's eye is narrow, letting in only a little light.

In dim light, the pupil is wide, letting in any available light, which is then reflected.

Feeling around

A cat's whiskers stick out from its cheeks, chin and forehead and help it to feel its way around in the dark. Whiskers are so sensitive that they can pick up a change in the weather or even a movement in the air.

Varying vision

Plant eaters need to see to the side as well as the front so they can keep a look out for predators while they graze. Most have eyes at the sides of their heads.

Deer – eyes at the side

INTERNET LINK
For a link to a website about amazing animal senses, go to **www.usborne-quicklinks.com**

A rabbit's tongue contains almost twice as many taste buds as a human's. Rabbits have around 17,000 taste buds while humans only have around 9,000.

Animals that hunt need to be able to focus clearly on the prey ahead of them as they give chase. Animals that live in trees need to be able to judge distances as they move from branch to branch. Both groups of animals have eyes at the front of their heads.

Lion – eyes in front

Best beak

When underwater, a platypus shuts its eyes, ears and nostrils. It relies only on its sensitive beak to help it find food. The beak picks up tiny pulses of electricity given out by its prey.

A platypus' beak is really a long snout covered with soft, leathery skin.

Eyes at the side (plant eaters)	Eyes at the front (hunters and tree-dwellers)
Cows	Apes
Deer	Bears
Giraffes	Cats
Mice	Dogs
Rabbits	Lions
Rats	Monkeys
Shrews	Raccoons

Nosy moles

A star-nosed mole spends most of its life underground feeling for food with the tentacles on its nose. These tentacles are almost six times more sensitive than your hand.

The pink tentacles on the mole's nose feel around for food.

Night Life

More types of mammal are active at night than during the day. These are called nocturnal mammals. There are several reasons why they prefer the night.

Foxes hunt at night because there are fewer other types of animal, such as birds of prey, looking for similar food.

Desert rats only go out at night, when the hot desert has cooled down.

Armadillos find it easier to hide from predators in the dark.

Nocturnal animal	Habitat
Armadillo	Forests and plains of North and South America
Bushbaby	African forests
Duck-billed platypus	Streams and rivers of East Australia
Gerbil	African and Asian deserts
Giant panda	Mountain forests of China
Hippopotamus	Lakes and rivers of East Africa
Lion	African grasslands
Northern fur seal	Northern Pacific Ocean
Raccoon	Deciduous forests of North America
Red fox	Forests and deserts of Europe, America, Africa and Asia
Rhinoceros	African grasslands
Sloth	Rainforests of South and Central America

Ear plugs

Bushbabies have sharp hearing to help them find food at night. During the day, they have to sleep with their ears folded inwards to block out the noises of the forest.

Bushbabies get their name from the noises they make at night, which sound like the cries of a newborn baby.

Bushbabies have huge eyes, but they rely more on hearing and smell.

INTERNET LINK
For a link to a website about animal night vision, go to
www.usborne-quicklinks.com

Hanging around

Flying foxes are really a type of bat. At night, they fly up to 65km in search of food. They spend their days hanging sleepily from trees, sometimes in extremely large groups called camps. On very hot days, they keep cool by fanning themselves with their wings.

Flying foxes can hang from a branch by one foot, but cannot stand upright because their legs are not strong enough.

At night, flying foxes look for fruit and nectar to eat.

Shy devil

Tasmanian devils can look and sound very fierce, but they are really quite shy. During the day, they usually hide in dense forests. At night, they roam long distances – up to 16km – in search of food.

This Tasmanian devil looks scary, but it is only making this face because it is frightened.

Night monkeys

Douroucoulis are the only nocturnal monkeys. They are sometimes called "owl monkeys" because of their huge eyes and the markings on their faces. They have very thick fur to keep them warm during cold nights.

Pygmy tarsiers are around 12cm long and their eyes are 1.5cm in diameter. That would be the same as a human having eyes the size of grapefruits.

Tarsiers need such big eyes to help them see in the dark.

Tarsiers' eyes do not move but their heads can turn nearly 360°.

Douroucoulis have large eyes to help them see in the dark.

Tops and Tails

Many animals use their heads as weapons or to send messages. Some have antlers or horns to help them do this.

Other animals use their tails to send messages. Tails can also help them to hold onto objects, or to move quickly.

A dolphin moves its tail up and down to help it move through the water.

Amazing antlers

Wapiti have the longest antlers. Their antlers can grow up to 1.8m wide (about the same length as a giraffe's neck) and weigh as much as 18kg (about as heavy as a three year old child).

A wapiti's antlers will grow around 2.5cm each day until they reach their full length in summer.

Hooded seals get their name because males can inflate part of their heads into a kind of hood. They can also blow out the skin inside their noses into a red balloon. They do this when they are excited or in danger.

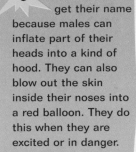

A hooded seal inflates its nose to twice the size of a football.

It can also blow the inside of its nostril out like a red balloon.

Wide load

The longest horns belong to the Indian water buffalo. A huge male, shot in 1955, had horns which measured 4.2m long from tip to tip – about twice as long as an elephant's trunk. Tame buffaloes usually have their horns trimmed.

A water buffalo's thick horns curve inwards and backwards.

Long horn

The white rhinoceros has two horns. The front horn can grow up to 1.6m long, which is about three times as long as a human arm. If the horn breaks off it will grow back at a rate of about 5mm a month.

The word rhinoceros actually means "nose horn".

Spider support

Spider monkeys have such strong tails that they can support their whole body weight with their tails alone.

INTERNET LINK

For a link to a website about tops, tails and other body parts, go to **www.usborne-quicklinks.com**

Long swatters

Asian elephants have the longest tails of all land mammals. They can grow up to 1.5m long – nearly as long as their trunks. Elephants use their tails as fly-swats.

Land mammals with the longest tails	Tail length
Asian elephant	1.5m
Leopard	1.4m
African elephant	1.3m
African buffalo	1.1m
Giraffe	1.1m
Red kangaroo	1m

A spider monkey uses its long tail as an extra limb as it moves from branch to branch.

Balancing act

When a kangaroo hops quickly it uses its tail for balance. When it hops slowly it uses its tail to push its hind legs off the ground, as though it was a fifth leg.

A red kangaroo stretches its tail out as it hops quickly.

The ground squirrel of the Kalahari Desert in South Africa keeps cool by angling its tail over its head like a parasol.

A ground squirrel on the move makes its own shade.

Tall tails

A dominant male lemur will walk with its head and tail held high.

When ring-tailed lemurs are walking along the ground in search of food, each keeps its striped tail raised high in the air. This shows the others where they are and keeps the group safely together.

Coats and Camouflage

Hair on an animal has a lot of uses:

It keeps an animal warm.

It can make it look bigger.

It can help it to hide.

It can protect it from injury.

Sloths move around so little that algae on the trees they hang from also begins to grow on their coats. The green algae helps to hide the sloth among the leaves.

Unlike any other mammal, a sloth's hair grows from its stomach down towards its back.

Marvellous mane

Young cheetahs have a thick mane of grey hair on their backs. The mane is about 8cm long and helps hide the cub among dry grasses and bushes. It also makes the cub look bigger and fiercer than it really is so it can scare away enemies.

By the time it is two years old, this cheetah's mane will have disappeared.

Taking a stand

A hyrax has a useful patch of hair on its back. The hairs are longer and a different colour to the rest of its coat. When the hyrax is threatened, the hairs stand on end to make it look bigger and more scary.

A happy hyrax

A scared hyrax

Warm coat

Arctic musk oxen have the longest fur. In winter, their outer layer of hair can grow up to 2m long. They also have a fleece undercoat. This helps them to survive in freezing temperatures as low as -60°C.

Without its warm, double-layered coat, a musk ox would freeze to death during winter.

INTERNET LINK

For a link to a website about animal camouflage, go to **www.usborne-quicklinks.com**

All a blur

Zebras' striped coats look blurred in the hazy heat of the African grasslands. This makes the zebra's outline harder to see from a distance.

It's hard to see where one zebra ends and the next begins...

Crouch for cover

When saiga antelopes sense danger, they crouch down and keep very still. Predators often mistake them for mounds of earth.

From a distance, this crouching antelope would be hard to spot.

Pangolins are the only mammals to have scales. The scales, like hedgehog quills, are made from hairs tightly joined together. Ordinary hairs grow between the scales and on the underside of a pangolin's body.

A pangolin raises its sharp-edged scales when it's under attack.

Seasonal changes

Arctic hares, foxes and stoats change their coats twice a year. They have white coats in winter so they don't stand out against the snow. In summer, their coats are brown or grey to blend in with rocks and earth.

An Arctic fox in summer...

...looks different from an Arctic fox in winter.

Blending in

Most big cats have yellow or brown fur with spotted or striped markings. At night or in patchy daylight this helps them to blend in with the light and shade of their surroundings.

This leopard has dark spots on its coat that blend in with the dappled light of the rainforest.

Fight and Flight

Most animals in the wild are always in danger of being eaten. Some have clever and unusual ways of defending themselves or escaping from predators.

Pin cushion

Porcupine quills can cause serious wounds. If attacked, a porcupine charges backwards, sticking quills into its attacker. As it moves away the quills are left behind.

This dog has a face full of quills. It made the mistake of attacking a porcupine.

A Canadian porcupine has about 30,000 quills, each up to 12cm long. Put end to end, they would reach a third of the way up Mount Everest.

Facing the enemy

If an enemy threatens, male musk oxen stand shoulder to shoulder. They line up in front of their calves and females, with their horns facing the attacker. A male ox steps out to do battle. If he falls, others follow one by one until the predator leaves or is killed.

Musk oxen form a wall-like defence.

Poison pals

Some animals use poison to kill or injure their attackers:

Platypus

Male duck-billed platypuses have poisoned spikes on their ankles, which they use to kick predators.

Poisonous shrew

Some types of shrew have poisons in their saliva. Shrew bites can paralyse small animals and cause painful skin swellings in people.

Solenodon

Solenodons are rare, shrew-like animals that live in Haiti and Cuba. Poison, strong enough to kill small animals, runs along grooves in their teeth.

Wood mice have disposable tails. If a mouse is grabbed by its tail, it sheds the skin that covers it. The bare tail that is left eventually shrivels and falls off.

This cat got less than he bargained for.

Warning signs

Some animals have warning signals which let other animals know about danger. They might also confuse or frighten a predator so that it does not attack.

You'll never catch me...

Springboks leap straight up into the air with arched backs. This is called pronking. It warns predators not to bother attacking such athletic creatures.

Hold your nose...

Secret weapon

A skunk's tail hides a very effective weapon. When threatened, the skunk lifts its tail and squirts out a horrible-smelling liquid from a gland beneath it. The terrible stink can be smelt up to 500m away.

INTERNET LINK

For a link to a website where you can learn about animal defences, go to **www.usborne-quicklinks.com**

Playing dead

The opossum fools its predators by pretending to be dead. When attacked, it rolls over and lies still, mouth open and eyes glazed over. The predator may then lose interest and go away.

No one knows if the opossum is playing dead or is simply paralysed with fear. After lying still for up to four hours, it looks around and, if the danger is over, comes back to life.

Faking death, or scared stiff?

Get ready to fight, or run...

Horses snort, raise their tails and prick up their ears to alert other horses to danger.

Listen to me!

Hyraxes make loud screaming warning calls.

Sending Messages

Animals have different ways to warn others of danger, mark their territory, call their young or find a mate – but most of them do it. They use smell, sight, sound and touch.

Hyenas "laugh" when afraid or excited.

Laughing hyenas

Hyenas don't really have a sense of humour. Only human beings can really laugh. But hyenas hunt in teams and use different noises to communicate. They growl, grunt, whine and yelp but also burst into noisy choruses that can sound like hysterical laughter.

A male orang-utan "burps" to keep other males out of his territory. He fills his throat pouch with air, swelling his face, and lets out a long call, ending with sighs – and bubbling burps.

Sea songs

Dolphins whistle to say hello.

Dolphins have a wide vocabulary of over 32 sounds. They use squeals, clicks, barks and whistles to keep in touch with each other.

Whales build up a series of sounds into songs. A song may last for up to thirty minutes. Whales have very loud voices – some are even louder then jet planes.

Humpback whales sing head down and tail up.

Loudest mammals	Sound level
Blue whale	188 decibels
Hippopotamus	115 decibels
Lion	114 decibels
Elephant	105 decibels
Bat	100 decibels
Howler monkey	90 decibels
Human (shouting)	70 decibels
Dog	50 decibels

Howler monkeys "sing" loudly to warn off predators.

Tail talk

Cats and dogs use their tails to show their feelings. A happy dog wags its tail, but if it's frightened, it puts its tail between its legs. An angry cat swishes its tail from side to side, but if it's happy, it holds its tail up in the air.

A happy cat   *A happy dog*

When two prairie dogs meet they "kiss" to find out if they know each other. If they don't, the intruder is driven away. If they do, they kiss again and start to groom each other.

Prairie dogs will stop to kiss even when rushing away from danger.

Speaking scents

Tenrecs are small, hedgehog-like creatures from Madagascar. They mark their territory with their body smell. They spit where they want to mark, rub their paws along their sides to pick up their smell, and then rub their paws in the spit.

Ring-tailed lemurs rub their bottoms on trees as they travel through the forest. They leave their scent to mark their trails so that the rest of the troop know where the lemur has been.

Tenrecs use saliva to mark their territory.

Ring-tailed lemurs leave a scent trail.

INTERNET LINK
For a link to a website where you can listen to a variety of animal noises, go to **www.usborne-quicklinks.com**

Making faces

Chimpanzees are among the very few animals that can make faces to show their feelings. They can show anger, happiness and interest very much like human beings. But if a chimp seems to be grinning by showing its teeth, it's probably not smiling but expressing fear.

This chimpanzee is making a "play face" – the expression it uses when it's playing, to show that it's happy.

This chimpanzee is unhappy.

This chimpanzee is afraid.

Animal Instincts

All animals have instincts – they automatically know how to do certain things to survive. Their instincts tell them how to find food, cope with extreme temperatures, breed and raise their young.

Shifting seasons

During the dry season, grassland zebras migrate to the hills and forests where there is more rain.

Zebras travel from grasslands to hills and back again.

In winter, prairie bison migrate to valleys and woods where they find shelter from the cold.

Bison travel from prairies to valleys and back again.

Migration marathons

Scientists think that some animals must have a sort of built-in compass. This is because they are able to migrate long distances, using the same routes every year without getting lost. They make these journeys to reach places where they can feed or breed.

Longest migrators	Distance travelled (there and back)	Colour
Grey whale	19,300km	⇨
Humpback whale	13,000km	⇨
Northern fur seal (male)	10,000km	⇨
Caribou	4,600km	⇨
Noctule bat	4,500km	⇨
European pipistrelle	3,800km	⇨

The longest mammal migrations are made by sea.

When grey whales migrate in winter, they make a 9,650km journey – about the same distance as from London to Tokyo. Starting from their feeding grounds in the Bering Straits, they travel south along the west coast of the USA to Mexico. The journey takes around 90 days. In the spring, they return north by the same route.

Fast asleep

Instinct tells some animals to sleep through the times of the year when food is scarce. While they sleep, their body temperature drops and their pulse and breathing rate slows.

Hibernation

Animals sleep through the cold winter months.

Hibernating bear

Longest hibernators	Months spent hibernating
Barrow ground squirrel	9
Marmot	7-8
Black bear	7
Hamster	6-7
European hedgehog	6

Aestivation

Animals sleep through the hot summer months.

Aestivating squirrel

Longest aestivators	Months spent aestivating
Uinta ground squirrel	9
Mojave ground squirrel	7
Yellow-bellied marmot	4
Desert jerboas	3
Cactus mouse	3

INTERNET LINK
For a link to a website about black bears in hibernation, go to **www.usborne-quicklinks.com**

! During hibernation, a marmot's body temperature drops to 10°C – low enough to kill a non-hibernating animal.

Useful instincts

Some animals' instincts can be very useful to people:

Dolphins instinctively find and pick up objects underwater. Navies use dolphins to help retrieve tools lost at sea.

Dogs instinctively chase and round up prey. Shepherds use dogs to help them herd sheep.

A single dog can control a large herd of sheep.

Pigs instinctively sniff out food. Farmers use pigs to help them find truffles (a type of mushroom).

The farmer has to grab the truffle quickly before the pig eats it.

Families and Herds

Many animals find it useful to live in groups. They can share food, look after each others' babies and groom each other. Groups of animals may hunt together so they can catch bigger prey. In larger groups, members may come and go. In smaller groups, they may stay together for longer, like a family.

The largest herd ever recorded was a group of over ten million springbok seen in southern Africa. The herd is said to have covered 5,360km^2 – over three times the area of London, England.

Springbok roam African grasslands.

Standing tall

While a family of meerkats feed or doze, one member of the group will watch out for danger. It stands on its hind legs to see over the long grass.

Alerted to danger, a meerkat family stands up to see what is approaching.

Group names

Some animal groups have very unusual names:

A clowder of cats
A leap of leopards
A pride of lions
A skulk of foxes
A labour of moles
A crash of rhinoceroses
A trip of goats
A shrewdness of apes

These lionesses are all members of the same group, called a pride.

Elephant funerals

When an elephant dies, the herd mourns and stays by the body for several days. They cover it with leaves and earth before they move on.

Animal	Approximate number in herd
Caribou	500,000-750,000
Bison	2,000-4,000
Springbok	1,000-3,000
Wapiti	300-400
Elephant	150-250
Wild horses	10-20
Zebra	5-20

During the summer, Bracken Cave in Texas, USA, is home to as many as 20 million Mexican free-tailed bats.

Naked mole rats huddle together to keep warm.

Sea support

If a sperm whale is injured, the other members of its group make a circle around it, supporting it near the surface so it can breathe.

An injured sperm whale is supported in what is called a "marguerite" formation, named after a type of daisy.

Rat palace

Naked mole rats live in colonies of up to 300. In each colony, only one female has all the babies. She is the "queen" and is guarded by a couple of male "soldier" rats.

The rest of the colony are workers. They live and work as a group, digging tunnels in chain-gangs and sleeping huddled together.

Mole rats work in a chain-gang, each one passing the freshly dug sand to the one behind.

Pack order

Wolves live in groups, called packs, of up to 20 members. Each wolf has its place in the pack's order of importance. You can tell how important a wolf is by the body language it shows to others in the pack.

Most important in pack

Second in importance in pack

Ordinary pack member

Least important in pack

INTERNET LINK
For a link to a website where you can meet the members of a wolf pack, go to **www.usborne-quicklinks.com**

35

Houses and Homes

The type of home an animal has depends on how much protection it needs from enemies and the weather. Many animals do not have fixed homes, but wander in search of food. Some live in one area, called a territory, which they defend against intruders.

Animal	Name of home
Badger	Sett
Bat	Roost
Bear	Den
Beaver	Lodge
Fox	Den or earth
Hare	Form
Muskrat	House
Otter	Holt
Rabbit	Burrow or warren
Squirrel	Drey

Master builders

Beavers build their homes out of wood. With its strong teeth, a beaver can fell a tree half a metre thick in just 15 minutes.

A beaver gnaws away at both sides of a tree trunk until the tree falls.

The largest beaver dam ever built was 700m long and strong enough to bear the weight of a person riding across it on horseback. It was built on the Jefferson River, USA.

Beaver lodges are made of sticks, logs, moss and grass.

First, the beavers build a dam of logs and mud across a river to form a pond.

In the pond, they build a dome-shaped wooden lodge the size of a large tent.

They build a living area inside, which is above water level. To reach it, they dig underwater tunnels.

Night nests

Chimpanzee nest

Orang-utans and chimpanzees build treetop nests to sleep in. They bend branches across to make a firm base and then weave smaller twigs into it. It only takes five minutes to build a nest.

Mouse house

Harvest mouse nest

A harvest mouse builds its nest among tall grasses. With its teeth, it splits blades of grass into thin strips and weaves them into a framework. The blades are still joined to the stalks, so the nest is very secure.

Prairie dog towns

Prairie dogs have the biggest burrows. They live in family groups called coteries. Areas where there are a lot of coteries are called prairie dog towns. The biggest prairie dog town ever found was in Texas, USA. About 160km wide and 400km long, the town was home to around 400 million prairie dogs.

A prairie dog burrow usually has a nursery, toilet, grass-lined nesting chamber, and a listening post near the surface.

A Russian mole rat digs using its teeth.

Russian mole rats are some of the fastest burrowers. They can shift 50 times their own weight in soil in around 20 minutes.

Interior decorating

Badgers are very house-proud. They live in setts made up of chambers with connecting tunnels. They line their bedrooms with bracken, moss and grass. On dry mornings, they drag huge piles of bedding outside to air in the sun.

Badgers close their eyes as they dig underground.

INTERNET LINK

For a link to a website where you can explore a variety of animal homes, go to **www.usborne-quicklinks.com**

Runners

Some animals are able to run very quickly to catch prey or escape from predators. Most fast-running animals run on their toes. Their ankles are half-way up their legs and their knees are close to their bodies.

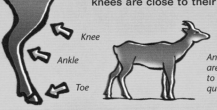

Knee

Ankle

Toe

An antelope's legs are long and thin to help it run quickly.

Pronghorn puff

Pronghorns can run at a speed of 45kph for up to 15 minutes. To stop them from running out of breath or getting too tired, they have well-developed lungs and a heart twice as big as that of other animals of a similar size.

A pronghorn can cover 6m in one stride.

6m

Non-slip feet

Like shoes, hoofs prevent slipping.

An animal's hoofs stick into the ground and stop it from slipping. They do the same job as spikes on running shoes.

Although they may look slow and clumsy, fully grown bears can run at a top speed of 40kph in short bursts. This is as fast as a galloping horse. Bears usually run quickly when chasing prey.

The fastest facts

Cheetahs are the fastest animals on land. They can only run quickly for short distances though, and have a rest after running around 500m.

• Cheetahs can reach a top speed of 115kph, which is as fast as a family car.

• Cheetahs can reach 72kph from a standstill in just two seconds.

• Cheetahs have flexible backbones which allow them to take giant 7m leaps.

A cheetah stretches its tail out for balance as it runs.

INTERNET LINK

For a link to website where you can watch a cheetah chase a gazelle, go to **www.usborne-quicklinks.com**

Let's dance

Madagascan sifakas have legs much longer than their arms, so running on all fours along the ground is impossible. Instead, they do a running hop on their back legs. They bounce from one foot to the other, holding their arms high in the air.

Sifakas spend most of their time in treetops and will only hop when they need to cross open ground.

Land waddlers

Both seals and sea lions are better at moving around in water than they are on land. On land or ice, seals can only drag themselves along on their bellies. Sea lions can turn their back flippers forward and waddle more easily than seals.

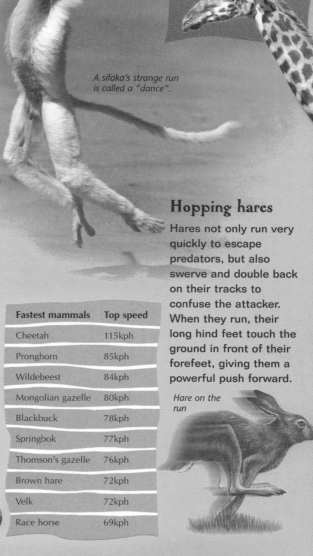

A sifaka's strange run is called a "dance".

Giraffes close their nostrils when they run to keep out the dust.

Giraffe with closed nostrils

Hopping hares

Hares not only run very quickly to escape predators, but also swerve and double back on their tracks to confuse the attacker. When they run, their long hind feet touch the ground in front of their forefeet, giving them a powerful push forward.

Hare on the run

A seal drags itself along.

A sea lion waddles.

Fastest mammals	Top speed
Cheetah	115kph
Pronghorn	85kph
Wildebeest	84kph
Mongolian gazelle	80kph
Blackbuck	78kph
Springbok	77kph
Thomson's gazelle	76kph
Brown hare	72kph
Velk	72kph
Race horse	69kph

39

Climbers

Some animals find food and shelter high up in mountains and trees. To reach these places, they need to be good climbers.

Helping hands

Asian tarsiers have pads on their long fingers and toes to help them grip branches.

Tarsier hand

Like people, African pottos can move their thumbs across the palms of their hands. They also have a short first finger. This gives them a very strong grip.

Pottos have specially adapted fingers.

Sloths have claws which hook onto branches as they hang upside-down in trees.

Sloths have hook-like claws.

! Adult spider monkeys sometimes stretch themselves between the branches of trees, making a bridge for their young to climb across.

A mother spider monkey bridges the gap for her baby.

Spiny tails

Some types of porcupine have spines underneath their tails which help them to grip tree trunks. Some also have non-slip pads on the soles of their feet.

Non-slip soles give porcupines extra grip.

INTERNET LINK

For a link to a website about rainforest animal climbers, go to **www.usborne-quicklinks.com**

A puma jumps out of a tree with its claws out to catch its unsuspecting prey.

Short cut

Most cats are good climbers but the puma has an even quicker way to get up and down trees. It is an excellent jumper. From a standstill, it can leap 7m – the height of four people – up into a tree. It can jump down to the ground from heights of up to 18m.

Rock climbing

Ibexes can climb incredibly steep mountain slopes and jump from rock to rock, leaping over huge gaps. Their hoofs have narrow edges that dig into cracks in the rocks and slightly hollow soles that help them cling to rocky slopes.

An ibex's sharp, hollow hoof can grip onto slippery and steep rocks.

When they sense danger, ibexes climb to the highest point they can reach.

Champion mountain climber

Tschingle, a beagle dog, accompanied her owner up 53 of the most difficult mountains in the Alps, 11 of which had never been climbed before. In 1875, she climbed Mont Blanc, the highest mountain in the Alps, and was made a member of the exclusive Alpine Club.

Quick climber

The fastest animal mountain climber is a type of mountain goat called a chamois. It lives in the Pyrenees and Alps in Europe and can climb 1,000m in only 15 minutes. A chamois could reach the top of Mount Everest in just over two hours.

Chamois can leap up to 6m from one rock to another.

Leopard larder

A leopard drags its prey up into trees, where it is out of the reach of other animals that might want to steal it. When it has climbed high enough, it eats what it can and stores the rest among the branches.

Highest living animals	Altitude
Marco Polo sheep	7,000m
Pika	6,100m
Snow leopard	6,000m
Yak	6,000m
Lesser mole rat	4,000m
Mountain gorilla	3,800m

Snow leopard

Animals in the Air

Some animals that live in trees have special flaps of skin that they use like wings. They don't fly, but glide from tree to tree as they search for food. Their front and back legs are joined by a flap of skin which acts as a parachute when they leap.

A colugo stretches its legs, and the skin between them, to glide.

Longest gliders	Length of glide
Yellow-bellied glider	115m
Giant flying squirrel	100m
Greater glider	100m
Colugo	90m
Southern flying squirrel	80m
Sugar glider	50m
Northern flying squirrel	50m
Feathertail glider	20m

INTERNET LINK

For a link to a website where you can see amazing gliding animals, go to **www.usborne-quicklinks.com**

Sugar gliders are very small – they are about the same length as a hamster.

Squirrel monkeys sometimes leap straight up into the air from the treetops to catch insects. They can jump up to 2.5m from a standing start.

Sweet gliders

A sugar glider gets its name from its sweet tooth. It likes sweet foods, such as tree sap and nectar. Sugar gliders are marsupials. This means that when a mother glides, she carries passengers – her babies are in a pouch on her stomach.

True flight

The only mammals that can really fly are bats. Their wings are made of thin, leathery skin supported by long, bony fingers.

Skin

Finger

This is the bat's thumb.

Asian flying fox

Asian flying foxes are the world's largest bats. They have a 1.8m wingspan – about the same wingspan as a golden eagle.

Hovering bats

Jamaican flower bats and tube-nosed fruit bats can hover. While hovering, they poke their long tongues into flowers to reach the nectar inside.

A bat hovers by flapping its wings very quickly.

Flying fishermen

The American hare-lipped bat is an expert fisherman. It flies low over ponds and lakes, using echo location* to sense a fish just below the surface. It then swoops down and rakes the water with its large claws. Once the fish is caught, the bat carries it away to a branch or rock to eat.

Hare-lipped bat on a successful fishing trip

Bat	Fastest speed	Similar speed to...
Mexican free-tailed bat	97kph	Car
Big brown bat	64kph	Racehorse
Red bat	60kph	Moped
Underwood's mastiff bat	40kph	Water skier
Little brown bat	19kph	In-line skater

* See page 20

Animals at Sea

Some animals, such as dolphins and whales, spend all their lives swimming in the sea.

Dolphins and whales swim using flippers and a tail fin, like this one.

Other sea animals, such as seals and walruses, live by the shore and spend some time on land.

Seals and walruses have flipper-like back legs to help them move on land.

Orcas can swim six times faster than the fastest human swimmer, reaching a top speed of about 48kph. They use their strong tails as propellers to speed them through the water.

Orca rocketing out of the sea

Sea unicorns

A narwhal only has two teeth. They grow straight forward from its top jaw. The male's left tooth is called a tusk. It grows in a spiral and can reach up to 2.5m long. Narwhals used to be killed for their tusks. Hunters would sell them as unicorn horns to be used in traditional medicines and to make ornaments.

No one is quite sure what narwhals use their tusks for.

Ocean spray

Whales can't breathe underwater, so have to come up to the surface to take a breath. They suck in fresh air and blow out used air through a blowhole in the top of their heads. The warm air they blow out is full of moisture, which forms a spray of water droplets.

A sperm whale's blowhole is on the left side of its head. This means that its spray shoots to the left.

A minke whale shoots a spray of water straight up into the air.

A right whale's blowhole is v-shaped and the spray shoots out in two streams.

INTERNET LINK
For a link to a website where you can learn about whales, go to **www.usborne-quicklinks.com**

Dolphin-napping

When a bottlenose dolphin goes to sleep, it closes only one eye so it can keep a look out for danger. It also shuts down only half of its brain. This is because it can't breathe automatically and has to decide when to come up to the surface for air. If it ever became fully unconscious, it would die. Every two hours, it swaps sides, resting the other side of its brain and closing the other eye. This pattern is called cat-napping.

Seal tears

On land, seals often look like they are crying. This is because they produce tears to keep their eyes wet and clean. In the sea, the tears get washed away, but on land they trickle down the seals' cheeks.

This seal's eyes are protected by thick, oily tears.

Adult walruses, which can weigh over a tonne, use their tusks to drag themselves over the land. The Latin name for walrus, *Odobenus*, actually means "the one that walks with its teeth".

This walrus is walking with its teeth.

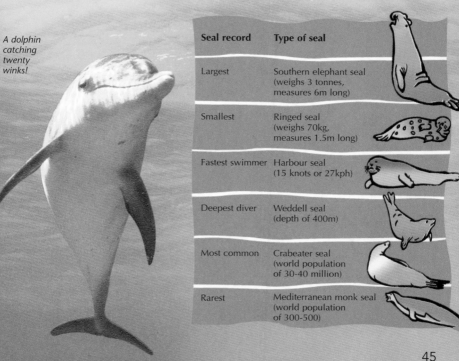

A dolphin catching twenty winks!

Seal record	Type of seal
Largest	Southern elephant seal (weighs 3 tonnes, measures 6m long)
Smallest	Ringed seal (weighs 70kg, measures 1.5m long)
Fastest swimmer	Harbour seal (15 knots or 27kph)
Deepest diver	Weddell seal (depth of 400m)
Most common	Crabeater seal (world population of 30-40 million)
Rarest	Mediterranean monk seal (world population of 300-500)

Island Animals

Many types of animal can only be found on certain islands. They are different to mainland animals because they have developed in isolation, over millions of years.

Crowned lemurs live only in Madagascar.

The older an island is, the more time its animals have had to change – Madagascar is the oldest island shown, Galápagos is the youngest.

Galápagos   Madagascar

—Australasia

Only in Galápagos	Only in Australasia	Only in Madagascar
		Fossas
		Greater big-footed mice
	Dingoes	Lemurs
Fernandina rice rats	Echidnas	Malagasy civets
Galápagos fur seals	Kangaroos	Malagasy giant rats
Galápagos red bats	Koalas	Narrow-striped mongooses
Galápagos sea lions	Numbats	Sucker-footed bats
Santa Fe rice rats	Tasmanian devils	Tenrecs
	Wombats	White-tipped tufted-tailed rats

All mixed up

A fossa has a nose like a dog, teeth like a leopard, and whiskers like an otter. It is only the size of a fox, but is Madagascar's largest predator.

Fossas jump from tree to tree, pouncing on lemurs, birds, frogs and lizards.

! The Madagascan sportive lemur gets its name because, when it is attacked, it raises its fists like a boxer and punches its enemy.

INTERNET LINK
For a link to a website about unique Australian animals,
go to www.usborne-quicklinks.com

A Tasmanian devil sneezes when it wants to challenge another devil to a fight.

Hairy seals

A Galápagos fur seal is very hairy. It has a thick coat made up of two layers of hair, one longer than the other. When a seal dives into the water, the long hairs fall over the small ones, trapping air between the two layers. The trapped air insulates the seal from the temperature of the water.

A Galápagos fur seal dives into the water.

Air is trapped between the two layers of hair in its coat.

As the seal swims, air bubbles stream from its coat.

Expert diggers

Wombats live in burrows in Australia and Tasmania. Their bodies are specially adapted for digging. Even their pouch faces backwards so that the baby carried inside is not showered with earth as its mother digs.

With its strong paws and claws, a wombat can dig as quickly as a person using a shovel.

While a mother wombat digs...

...its baby looks out from its pouch, facing away from the flying dirt.

Tree hopping

In Australia and Papua New Guinea, some types of kangaroo live in trees. They move around by jumping between branches and can leap distances up to 15m. When they are on the ground, they can't jump so walk on all fours.

This mother tree kangaroo will carry her baby in her pouch for as long as ten months.

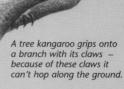

A tree kangaroo grips onto a branch with its claws – because of these claws it can't hop along the ground.

Animals on Ice

Animals that live in very cold places have special ways of keeping warm, finding food and moving around on ice and snow.

Black and white

A polar bear's coat acts like a thick, warm sweater. It is made of hollow hairs. Sunlight warms the air trapped in the hairs.

Beneath a polar bear's coat, its skin is black. Sunlight passes through the hairs and is then absorbed by the black skin. This also helps to keep the bear warm.

This polar bear's skin is actually black.

Sunlight passes through its hairs and is absorbed by its black skin.

Polar bears are strong swimmers but prefer to get around by using pieces of ice as rafts.

Floating on a raft uses much less energy than swimming.

Snowshoes

Snowshoe rabbits get their name from their broad feet. These act like snowshoes and stop the rabbits sinking in the deep snow. Long hairs grow on the sides of their feet and between their toes. The hairs keep their feet warm and help them to grip the frozen ground. They can jump over 5m in one hop.

Snowshoe rabbit

INTERNET LINK

For a link to a website where you can play a game about animals on ice, go to **www.usborne-quicklinks.com**

Scraping snow

When snow covers the ground, caribou scrape holes in it to eat the lichen plants underneath. How the caribou know where to dig is a mystery. Perhaps they can smell the lichen under the snow.

Caribou use their feet and antlers to dig up food.

Mammals with coldest homes	Lives in temperatures as low as...
Arctic wolf	-75°C
Polar bear	-65°C
Musk ox	-60°C
Husky dog	-45°C
Caribou	-40°C

Musk ox

Cool patches

Vicuñas live high up in the snow-covered South American mountains. Despite the freezing temperatures, vicuñas can overheat because their coats are so warm. They have bare patches on their legs which they turn towards the wind to help them cool down.

Vicuñas

Bath time for a macaque

Japanese macaques keep warm by taking hot baths. During the winter, they spend most of their time sitting in hot, volcanic springs, often with the water right up to their necks.

Frozen fox food

In summer, Arctic foxes bury eggs and other food under the ground. When winter comes, they dig through the snow and ice to get to the deep-frozen food.

Arctic fox digging for eggs in its deep-freeze

Arctic foxes also get food by listening out for small animals under the snow. When they hear one, they jump up and down to break through the snow. Once the snow is broken, they can grab their prey.

Arctic fox trying to break the ice to reach a group of lemmings hiding beneath

49

Desert Animals

Deserts are very dry places that have less than 25cm of rain a year. Hardly any plants grow there. Desert animals need ways to keep cool and to find enough to eat and drink in their hot, dry surroundings.

You can see the blood vessels in this jack rabbit's ear.

Big ears

A jack rabbit uses its big ears to keep cool. The hot blood flowing in blood vessels near the surface is cooled by the air around them. To catch a slightly cooler breeze, the rabbit faces north.

Air traps

A desert that is very hot by day can become very cold at night. Some desert animals have fur on their bodies that traps a layer of air. This layer insulates them from extreme heat or cold.

Fur insulates the skin from heat during the day...

Hot air

Skin

...and from cold at night.

Cold air

Desert wallabies and kangaroos use their own spit to keep themselves cool. When it is very hot, they pant and make a lot of saliva, which they lick all over themselves. As it evaporates, the saliva cools the animal down.

Animals of the Sahara Desert	Animals of the Gobi Desert	Animals of the Arabian Desert	Animals of the Mojave Desert	Animals of the Great Victoria Desert
Addax	Mongolian gerbil	Arabian oryx	Jack rabbit	Kangaroo
Fennec fox	Gazelle	Striped hyena	Coyote	Wallaby
Jerboa	Bactrian camel (two humps)	Dromedary (camel with one hump)	Mojave ground squirrel	Dingo
Desert hedgehog	Gobi bear	Arabian gazelle	Bighorn sheep	Bilby

Underground cool

Some small desert animals spend their days underground to avoid the heat. Just 10cm below ground, the temperature can be up to 20° cooler than on the surface.

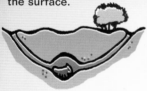

A ground squirrel may burrow up to 1m below the ground.

Storage space

A camel can survive for nine days without water and 33 days without food. The secret is in its hump, which stores fat that can be used when there is no food. When it reaches water, a camel can drink 123 litres in ten minutes – about two-thirds of a bathtub full.

A camel's hump can weigh up to 35kg – as much as a seven year old child.

Catching its breath

Jerboas save the moisture in their breath. They spend their days sleeping inside sealed burrows with their bushy tails over their mouths, to keep the moisture in.

A jerboa catching its breath

No drinking

The addax, a rare antelope, never needs to drink. It gets all its moisture from the plants it eats. It is one of the very few large animals that is able to survive in the driest parts of the southern Sahara desert.

Jerboas even eat their own droppings for the moisture and vitamins they still contain.

The addax is one of the world's rarest mammals.

INTERNET LINK
For a link to a website about the animals of the Sahara desert, go to **www.usborne-quicklinks.com**

Rainforest Animals

Rainforests grow near the equator where it is always warm and rains nearly every day. The different levels of the rainforest are full of different types of animal.

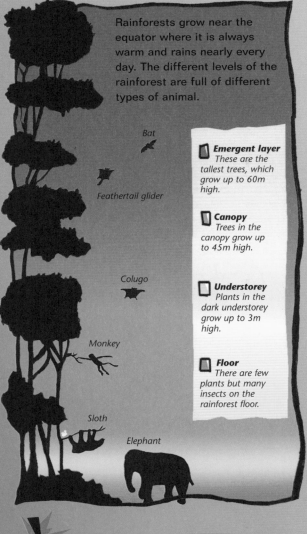

Bat

Feathertail glider

Colugo

Monkey

Sloth

Elephant

Emergent layer
These are the tallest trees, which grow up to 60m high.

Canopy
Trees in the canopy grow up to 45m high.

Understorey
Plants in the dark understorey grow up to 3m high.

Floor
There are few plants but many insects on the rainforest floor.

During the rainy season, the Amazon River floods parts of the forest. Pink Amazon River dolphins can be seen swimming through the underwater trees.

Eating insects

Insect-eating animals, even big ones, find plenty to eat on the rainforest floor.

Aye-ayes have such good ears that they can hear insect grubs tunnelling in dead wood and fallen branches. They bite holes in the wood and use their long, skinny fingers to scrape out the grubs.

An aye-aye listens for its next meal.

Sun bears use their big paws to scoop ants out of ants' nests. Their tongues are long enough to poke into holes in logs, reaching insects hidden inside.

A sun bear licks insects off its paws.

Bat tents

Some fruit bats make leaf "tents", which protect them from predators and the weather.

INTERNET LINK

For a link to a website where you can go on a rainforest adventure, go to www.usborne-quicklinks.com

A fruit bat chews leaves at the base near the stem.

The leaves collapse to form a shelter.

Animals of the Asian rainforests	Animals of the South American rainforests	Animals of the African rainforests
Bengal tiger	Giant anteater	Bushbaby
Common palm civet	Marmoset	Chimpanzee
Orang-utan	Panther	Gorilla
Silvery gibbon	Squirrel monkey	Hippopotamus
Sumatran rhinoceros	Tapir	Hyrax

Killer otters

Giant otters are among the most successful predators in the Brazilian rainforest and have even been known to kill anacondas. People are their only predators.

Wake up call

Howler monkeys howl at regular times – their loud calls "wake up" the rainforest in the morning and "put it to bed" at night. Sometimes they howl just before it rains, like a sort of weather forecast.

Water pigs

Capybaras look like a cross between a beaver and a pig. Their scientific name, *Hydrochoerus*, means "water pig". They live along ponds and rivers in rainforests and have partially webbed feet. When threatened, they will often jump in the water and hide.

Capybaras swim well but walk clumsily because of their webbed feet.

Howler monkeys are the loudest rainforest animals.

Howler monkeys sometimes tease jaguars – but from a safe distance up in the trees. They throw sticks at the jaguar below. The jaguar, meanwhile, waits for an unfortunate howler to slip and fall.

Capybaras keep cool in the water.

Grassland Animals

Grasslands are open and windy areas of land where grasses and low bushes grow. For most of the year, grasslands are very dry. Lots of different plant eaters live on grasslands and are hunted by meat eaters.

Browsers (eat leaves)	Grazers (eat grass)	Predators (eat meat)
Giraffes	Zebras	Lions
Elephants	Wildebeest	Cheetahs
Black rhinoceroses	White rhinoceroses	Leopards
Kudus	Hippopotamuses	Hunting dogs
Gerenuks	Bison	Hyenas
	Warthogs	Servals

This kudu is running for its life.

This lion is about to catch its next meal.

Working together

Hunting dogs, hyenas and lions usually chase animals that are larger and faster than them. To catch their prey, they work together in pairs or small groups. Once the animal is caught, the group shares the food.

Hunting dogs on the look-out for prey

In and out

A warthog always enters its burrow backwards, so it can fight off enemies with its tusks while backing in. In the mornings, it bursts out of its burrow at top speed to get a running start on any enemies that may be watching.

A warthog never turns its back on an enemy.

Bat-eared foxes have such excellent hearing that they can even hear termites moving underground. They then dig up the termites and eat them.

This fox's ears pick up the tiniest sounds.

Grassland groups

Many animals roam the grassland in groups.
The groups are organized in different ways:

Lion prides are led by a few males whose job is to protect the females. Females hunt and take care of the cubs.

Baboon troops are led by an older male. He keeps everyone together and defends his troop if it is attacked.

Females and cubs of a lion pride

Leader of a baboon troop

Wildebeest

Wildebeest herds are always on the move. They have no leader and members come and go as they please.

Gerenuks are the only hoofed animals that can stand on their hind legs.

A gerenuk balances on its hind legs to reach up for a snack.

INTERNET LINK
For a link to a website where you can become a grassland wildlife photographer, go to **www.usborne-quicklinks.com**

Shelter below

There are not many places to hide or shelter from the weather on grasslands, so many small animals live underground. Some come up to the surface to find food but others spend all their lives underground.

• Mole rats live under the African grasslands.

• Black-bellied hamsters live under the Asian grasslands.

• Gophers live under the prairies – the North American grasslands.

• Maras live under the pampas – the South American grasslands.

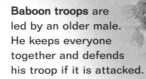

Animals in Danger

When a type of animal dies out, is it said to be extinct. If it is likely to die out unless we take action, it is said to be threatened or endangered.

In parts of Africa, people are trying to save rare rhinos by sawing off their horns so that hunters will leave them alone. Rhinos are hunted so that their horns can be used in traditional medicines.

Rhino with two sawn-off horns

Growing number

In the 1970s, there were only 200 golden lion tamarins in the wild. The places where they lived were being damaged, and they were being hunted and captured for the pet trade, zoos and medical research. Now they live in protected parts of the rainforest and it is illegal to hunt them. By 2001, their number had grown to 1,000.

Golden lion tamarin

Small world

A mountain gorilla in its rainforest home

Mountain gorillas must be very attached to their natural habitat, as none have ever survived in captivity. There are only around 600 mountain gorillas left in the world and they all live in an area of African rainforest measuring just 740km^2.

Recently extinct animals	Last seen...
Pyrean ibex	2000
Javan tiger	1980
Barbary lion	1960
Japanese sea lion	1951
Tasmanian tiger-wolf	1936
Martinique muskrat	1902
Quagga	1883

	Most endangered mammals	Found in...	Population in wild (2001)
1	Baiji dolphin	China	Fewer than 40
2	Seychelles sheath-tailed bat	Seychelles	Fewer than 50
3	Javan rhinoceros	Indonesia; Vietnam	Fewer than 60
4	Northern hairy-nosed wombat	Australia	60
5	Hisipid hare	India; Nepal	110
6	Black-footed ferret	North America	Fewer than 200
7	Tonkin snub-nosed monkey	Vietnam	200
8	Kouprey	Cambodia	Fewer than 250
9	Yellow-tailed woolly monkey	Peru	Fewer than 250
10	Visayan spotted deer	Philippines	Fewer than 500

Ferret FM

When the black-footed ferret population was down to just 18, scientists began to breed them in captivity. Today, when young ferrets are released into the wild, they are fitted with radio collars so that people can keep track of them.

Signals transmitted from the radio collar are picked up by a receiver.

Dangerous waters

Speedboats are the greatest threat to rare manatees, which swim slowly, near the surface of the water. In one year, 218 manatees in the USA were killed and many more were injured when hit by boats.

INTERNET LINK
For a link to a website where you can visit an endangered animal hotel, go to **www.usborne-quicklinks.com**

In the 1970s, ivory was more valuable than gold. This led to thousands of elephants being killed for their ivory tusks. Hunting elephants is now illegal in most countries and there are many national parks and reserves where elephants are protected.

Hunters killed the elephants with the biggest tusks.

57

Biome Map

A biome is a large area with one main type of climate and one main type of vegetation. This map shows the seven principal biomes and some of the animals found in them.

Brown bear

Fox

ASIA

EUROPE

AFRICA

Ibex

African elephant

AUSTRALASIA

Camel

Sperm whale

Kangaroo

Key
- Poles and tundra
- Deserts
- Grasslands
- Mountains
- Coniferous forests
- Deciduous forests
- Rainforests

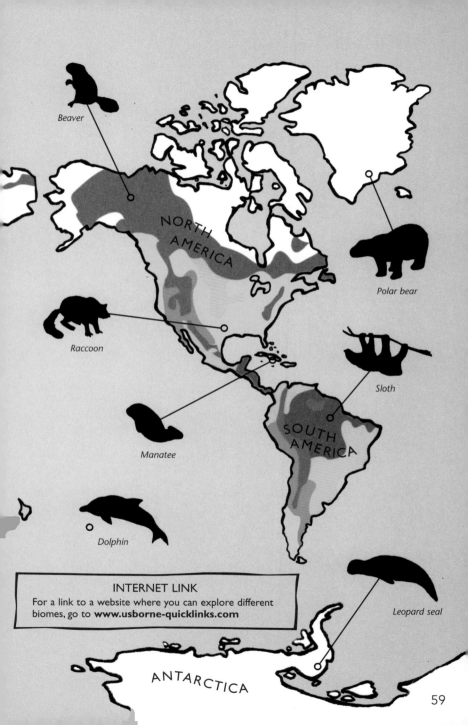

Beaver

NORTH AMERICA

Polar bear

Raccoon

Sloth

Manatee

SOUTH AMERICA

Dolphin

INTERNET LINK
For a link to a website where you can explore different biomes, go to www.usborne-quicklinks.com

Leopard seal

ANTARCTICA

Animals Quiz

So, now you've taken a walk on the wild side, how much can you remember about the animal world? Do you know your tarsiers from your tenrecs? Take our quiz to find out how much of an expert you really are...

Answers on page 64

1 A baby llama is called a:

A puggle

B leveret

C cria

D whelp

(See page 6)

2 A whale's baleen is:

A on its tail

B in its mouth

C under its fins

D in its blowhole

(See page 19)

3 Scientists count the ear plug rings on whales and dolphins to find out:

A how good its hearing is

B what it eats

C whether it's a male or a female

D how old it is

(See page 10)

4 The animal with the heaviest brain is the:

A blue whale

B sperm whale

C African elephant

D polar bear

(See page 13)

5 Koalas eat:

A bamboo

B oak

C eucalyptus

D pine

(See page 16)

6 Which of these animals isn't a scavenger?

A rhino

B lion

C hyena

D hunting dog

(See page 17)

7 Which two animals use echo location to sense where an object is?

A bats and rabbits

B rabbits and moles

C bats and dolphins

D dolphins and moles

(See page 20)

8 Which animal's heart beats faster than a human's?

A whale

B horse

C cow

D rabbit

(See page 14)

9 Flying foxes are really a type of:

A fox

B badger

C bat

D squirrel

(See page 23)

10 A hooded seal's nose is:

A spotted

B inflatable

C green

D very long

(See page 24)

11 Elephants use their tails to:

A pick up objects

B shade them from the sun

C help them balance

D swat flies

(See page 25)

12 The only mammal to have hairy scales is the:

A armadillo

B pangolin

C capybara

D anteater

(See page 27)

13 A wood mouse escapes from a predator by:

A squirting it with a foul-smelling liquid

B shedding its tail skin

C pricking it with a poisonous ankle spike

D pretending to be dead

(See page 29)

14 When an animal is hibernating, its:

A pulse speeds up and its temperature drops

B pulse slows and its temperature rises

C pulse speeds up and its temperature rises

D pulse slows and its temperature drops

(See page 33)

15 Which of these animals make faces to show their feelings?

A horses

B prairie dogs

C chimpanzees

D rabbits

(See page 31)

16 A group of goats is called a:

A shrewdness

B crash

C skulk

D trip

(See page 34)

17 Male hippos show their teeth when they:

A are happy

B want to warn off rivals

C are scared

D are hungry

(See page 8)

18 A nocturnal animal:

A only eats meat

B only eat plants

C has eyes at the side of its head

D is more active at night than during the day

(See page 22)

19 Most fast-running animals have:

A knees close to their bodies

B knees half-way up their legs

C knees close to their toes

D no knees

(See page 38)

20 The fastest animal mountain-climber is the:

A Marco Polo sheep

B pika

C snow leopard

D chamois

(See page 41)

21 The only mammals that can truly fly are:

A sugar gliders

B flying squirrels

C bats

D colugos

(See page 43)

22 The speediest seal is the:

A ringed seal

B crabeater seal

C Southern elephant seal

D harbour seal

(See page 45)

23 Which of these animals isn't found in Madagascar?

A tenrec

B echidna

C lemur

D fossa

(See page 46)

24 A polar bear's skin is:

A white

B brown

C black

D blue

(See page 48)

25 A jack rabbit keeps cool by:

A losing heat through its big ears

B covering itself in spit

C burrowing underground

D taking cold baths

(See page 50)

26 The only predators of giant otters are:

A anacondas

B humans

C sun bears

D howler monkeys

(See page 53)

27 Which one these animals isn't a browser?

A giraffe

B kudu

C zebra

D elephant

(See page 54)

28 The greatest threat to manatees are:

A sharks

B hunters

C jellyfish

D speedboats

(See page 57)

29 Most of Europe's natural vegetation is:

A deciduous forest

B coniferous forest

C rainforest

D grassland

(See page 58)

30 What does a tarsier have to help it grip onto branches?

A pads on its fingers

B spikes on its tail

C hook-like claws

D short first fingers

(See page 40)

Glossary

aestivation A deep sleep or time of inactivity to save energy and keep cool during very hot and dry weather.

algae Very simple, plant-like organisms that have no roots or leaves, ranging in size from one-celled plankton to giant seaweed.

baleen Fringes of keratin that hang inside a whale's mouth.

biome A large area with one main type of climate and one main type of vegetation.

blood vessel A tube in an animal's body through which blood flows.

blowhole An opening through which whales and dolphins breathe, located at the top of their heads.

breeding When a male and female animal join together to produce young.

browsers Animals that eat leaves.

burrow A hole or tunnel dug in the ground by a small animal.

camouflage Special colourings or markings that help animals to disguise themselves.

captivity Being in captivity is being trapped in a small space.

colony A group of animals of the same type that live together in one place.

coniferous forests Forests made up of narrow-leaved, evergreen trees.

continents Earth's great land masses: Asia, Africa, North and South America, Europe, Australiasia and Antarctica.

deciduous forests Forests made up of trees that lose their leaves before winter.

desert An area of land where there is very little rain and few plants.

digestion When food is broken down and its nutrients absorbed inside an animal's body.

echo location Using sound waves to work out where objects are and how big they are.

endangered A species of animal that is at risk of dying out.

equator An imaginary line drawn around the middle of the Earth an equal distance from the North and South Pole.

evaporate When a liquid is changed into a gas, usually as a result of heating.

extinct An animal that no longer exists. An animal becomes officially extinct if there have been no certain records of it for 50 years.

grasslands Open and windy areas of land where grasses and low bushes grow.

gravity A force that pulls objects towards the Earth's core.

grazers Animals that eat grass.

groom To clean an animal, usually by licking or picking through its fur.

habitat The natural surroundings in which an animal or plant lives.

herd A group of animals that live and feed together.

hibernation A deep sleep or time of inactivity to save energy during the cold winter months.

hoof Horny part of an animal's foot.

horn Growth on an animal's head, made from keratin.

hover To stay in one place in the air.

instinct The way an animal naturally behaves, without having to learn or think about it.

insulate To cover something to stop it from getting too cold or too hot.

ivory The hard, smooth substance that makes up elephants' tusks.

keratin The substance that makes up hair, horn and fingernails.

krill Small, shrimp-like ocean creatures.

lichen Simple plants that grows on rocks and tree trunks, made up of fungi and algae living together.

life cycle The series of changes an animal goes through during its life.

lifespan The length of time for which an animal lives.

mammals A group of warm-blooded animals that have hair and feed their young on milk from their bodies.

marsupials Mammals with pouches, such as kangaroos and koalas.

mate One of a pair of animals that come together to breed.

maturity Being fully grown physically.

migrate To travel to a different place in order to live there for a season.

mountain A raised part of the Earth's surface, much larger than a hill, the top of which might be covered in snow.

muzzle The forward, projecting part of the head of certain animals, such as dogs, including the mouth, jaws and nose.

nocturnal animal An animal that is most active at night.

Poles The two points at the most northern and most southern ends of the Earth.

population The total number of animals in a specific area.

prairie A wide area of flat land without trees found in Canada or USA.

predators Animals that hunt and eat other animals.

prey An animal that is hunted for food by other animals.

pulse The regular beating of an animal's heart.

quill A sharp hollow spine on a porcupine or hedgehog.

rainforests Dense, warm forests that have at least 2.5m of rainfall each year.

saliva The liquid produced inside an animal's mouth to keep the mouth wet and to help prepare food for digestion.

scavengers Animals that feed on dead animals that they have not killed themselves.

sense The ability to understand, recognize, value or react to an external stimulus.

teat A nipple on a female mammal's body through which milk is passed.

territory An area that an animal "owns" and defends against intruders.

tundra A large area of land where the ground is frozen in winter.

vitamin Any of a group of natural substances which are necessary in small amounts for the growth and good health of an animal's body.

warm-blooded Animals that can control their own body temperature so it always stays the same, whatever the temperature of their surroundings.

Acknowledgements

Every effort has been made to trace the copyright holders of the material in this book. If any rights have been omitted, the publishers offer to rectify this in any subsequent editions following notification. The publishers are grateful to the following organizations and individuals for their permission to reproduce material (t=top, m=middle, b=bottom, l=left, r=right):

AnimalsAnimals: 15b Wegner, Jorg & Petra/AnimalsAnimals/Earth Scenes; 35t Mendez, Raymond/AnimalsAnimals/Earth Scenes
Corbis: 1 Nigel J. Dennis, Gallo Images/CORBIS; 2-3 George D. Lepp/CORBIS; 6b John Conrad/CORBIS; 8b Gallo Images/CORBIS; 11br Bettmann/CORBIS; 17b Tom Brakefield/CORBIS; 20r James L. Amos/CORBIS; 22bl Anthony Bannister, Gallo Images/CORBIS; 23tm Theo Allofs/CORBIS; 24b Raymond Gehman/CORBIS; 26bm Paul A. Souders/CORBIS, mr Kennan Ward/CORBIS; 28tm Gunter Marx Photography/CORBIS; 33b Owen Franken/CORBIS; 36b Rose Hartman/CORBIS; 41tr Giry Daniel/CORBIS SYGMA; 46b Chris Hellier/CORBIS; 51br Steve Kaufman/CORBIS; 53b Kevin Schafer/CORBIS; 54m Gallo Images/CORBIS; 56tr Terry Whittaker, Frank Lane Picture Agency/CORBIS
Digital Vision: 8ml; 9tr, ml; 13mr; 16bl; 18b; 27b, tl; 30tr; 34m, mr, bl; 39tr; 45bl; 46tr; 50t; 55tl, tm
Husar: 48t Lisa and Mike Husar/TeamHusar.com
Getty Images: 24mr Anup Shah/Getty Images; 31br Getty Images/PhotoDisc
Ken Catania: 21b Ken Catania, Vanderbilt University, Nashville, Tennessee
Nature Picture Library: 17ml Jeff Foott/Nature Picture Library
Natural History Photographic Agency: 39tm Andy Rouse/NHPA
Science Photo Library: 43m Merlin Tuttle/Science Photo Library

Additional illustrators Ian Jackson, Rachel Lockwood, Malcolm McGregor, Chris Shields, David Wright

Additional designer Michael Hill

Quiz answers
1C, 2B, 3D, 4B, 5C, 6A, 7C, 8D, 9C, 10B, 11D, 12B, 13B, 14D, 15C, 16D, 17B, 18D, 19A, 20D, 21C, 22D, 23B, 24C, 25A, 26B, 27C, 28D, 29A, 30A

SEAS AND
OCEANS

SEAS AND OCEANS

Phillip Clarke

Designed by
Karen Tomlins and Luke Sargent

Digital imagery by Keith Furnival

Consultants: **Dr Ben Wigham,**
Southampton Oceanography Centre
and H.M. Hignett

Internet Links

Throughout this book, we have suggested interesting websites where you can find out more about the oceans. To visit the sites, go to the **Usborne Quicklinks website** at **www.usborne-quicklinks.com** and type the keywords "book of facts". There you will find links to click on to take you to all the sites. Here are some of the things you can do on the websites:

 See an undersea world through a live webcam.

 Hunt for giant squid in the deep sea in an interactive animation.

 Take a virtual tour of a huge cargo ship.

 See an animated map of the voyages of early sea explorers.

 See photographs of beautiful coral reefs.

Computer not essential

If you don't have access to the Internet, don't worry. This book is complete on its own.

Seas and Oceans Contents

Salty Seas

Over two-thirds of the Earth is covered in water. Together, the Pacific, Atlantic, Indian, Southern and Arctic Oceans form a continuous stretch of water that covers an area nine times that of the Moon's surface.

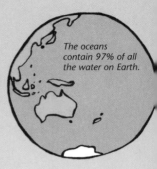

The oceans contain 97% of all the water on Earth.

The five oceans

Arctic Ocean

Pacific Ocean

Atlantic Ocean

Pacific Ocean

Indian Ocean

Southern Ocean

Why is the sea blue?

On sunny days, sea water looks blue because it reflects blue light rays from the Sun. The Yellow Sea, near China, gets its name from yellow clay washed down by rivers. The Black Sea, near Russia, is coloured by black mud.

Oceans by area	
Pacific Ocean	155,557,000km²
Atlantic Ocean	76,762,000km²
Indian Ocean	68,556,000km²
Southern Ocean	20,327,000km²
Arctic Ocean	14,056,000km²

The White Sea, north of Russia, is so called because it is covered in ice for 200 days a year.

Ocean birth

Soon after the Earth was formed, 4,600 million years ago, the ocean began to take shape. Water vapour rose from the Earth's hot surface. As it cooled, it formed storm clouds, and the first rain fell, creating the first, boiling ocean.

Storms raged for thousands of years to form the first ocean.

There is enough salt in the oceans to cover the land with a layer 150m deep. Some of this salt comes from underwater volcanoes, but most is from the land. Rain dissolves salt in the rocks; rivers carry it to the sea.

Largest seas	Area
Weddell Sea (Southern Ocean)	8,000,000km^2
Arabian Sea (Indian Ocean)	7,456,000km^2
South China Sea (Pacific Ocean)	2,974,000km^2
Mediterranean Sea (Atlantic Ocean)	2,505,000km^2
Barents Sea (Arctic Ocean)	1,300,000km^2

INTERNET LINKS

For links to websites where you can find an interactive map of the world's seas and oceans, an animation of the water cycle, or listen to undersea sounds, go to **www.usborne-quicklinks.com**

Ocean or sea?

A sea is an area within an ocean. Some seas are part of the open ocean, such as the Sargasso Sea in the Atlantic. Others, such as the South China Sea, are partly landlocked.

3,000 million years ago, tiny cells in the sea, called blue-green bacteria, started using sunlight to make their food, and giving off oxygen as they did so. Over millions of years, Earth's atmosphere gained enough oxygen for animals – like us – to survive.

Blue-green bacteria are still around today.

The South China Sea is shown in darker blue.

China

Philippines

Dolphins live in most of the world's oceans. They can swim at speeds of up to 40kph.

Speedy sound

Sound travels more than four times faster through sea water than through air. It took just 144 minutes for the sound of an undersea explosion off Australia to reach Bermuda, halfway round the world.

Everlasting water

There is no new water on Earth. The same water moves from the oceans to the sky to the land. Rivers return the water to the oceans, and the cycle goes on.

Water just goes round and round.

Restless Oceans

The Earth's hard crust is in seven large pieces, and many smaller ones, called plates. These lie like giant rafts on the softer rock layer beneath. As plates collide or drift apart, they alter the oceans' shape and size.

Sliding under

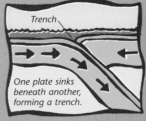

One plate sinks beneath another, forming a trench.

Where undersea plates collide, one plate is often pushed under another and melts back into the Earth. These areas, called subduction zones, form long, narrow trenches in the seabed, over 10km deep.

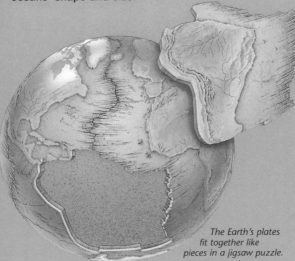

The Earth's plates fit together like pieces in a jigsaw puzzle.

The Himalayas were once part of the sea floor. Today, they are 500km from the sea. They formed 40 million years ago, when India drifted north and crashed into Asia, pushing seabed rocks 8km into the air.

Fossil seashells like this have been found on Mount Everest.

Ancient oceans

About 170 million years ago, all the continents formed one landmass, called Pangaea. Around it lay a vast ocean called Panthalassa.

As Pangaea split into continents, the Indian, Atlantic and Southern Oceans were formed. Panthalassa became the Pacific Ocean.

Part of Panthalassa jutted into the mainland of Pangaea, forming the Tethys Sea.

The movement of the Earth's plates began to form the oceans we know today.

Salt lake

About six million years ago, plates colliding together caused the Mediterranean Sea to become cut off from the oceans:

The Mediterranean Sea was cut off from the oceans as Morocco and Spain collided.

In about 1,000 years the water dried up, leaving the sea bottom caked in a layer of salt 1km thick.

Then the Atlantic Ocean rose. Over 100 years, water flowed back to the sea, in the biggest waterfall ever.

Island birth

In November 1963, an underwater volcano erupted near Iceland and formed a new island called Surtsey. Four days later, Surtsey was 61m long. Within 18 months the first leafy green plant was growing on the island.

When the eruption that created Surtsey began, it was thought to be a ship on fire.

Magma poured from the volcano, and cooled in the water, forming new rock.

Seaquakes

There are about a million earthquakes a year. Many happen underwater around the Pacific Ocean. The deepest seaquakes occur beneath ocean trenches, up to 750km below sea level. Most are never felt.

! In the last Ice Age, 18,000 years ago, it was possible to walk from England to France. The sea level was over 120m lower than it is today. Since then, sea level has risen by about 8cm every 100 years.

INTERNET LINKS

To find links to websites about how the oceans were formed, go to **www.usborne-quicklinks.com**

Icebergs are formed when chunks break off the Antarctic ice sheet.

Seafloor spread

New seafloor crust is always being made. As undersea plates separate, liquid rock, known as magma, rises to fill the gap and solidifies into mountains. The ocean floor grows about 4cm wider every year.

Flood warning

Today, ice covers about a tenth of the Earth. A temperature rise of 4°C could melt all the ice and raise sea level by about 70m. Coastal cities, such as Sydney, Tokyo and New York, would be drowned.

Under the Sea

Land

Seascape

Under the sea, the landscape is as varied as on land. Parts of this seascape have different names, according to their depth below sea level.

Continental margin

Continental shelf (less than 200m deep)

Continental slope (less than 2.5km deep)

Continental rise (less than 4km deep)

Abyssal plain (over 4km deep)

On the shelf

The continental shelf varies in how far it extends from the shore: from 1km on South America's Pacific coast to 1,200km around northern Siberia. Most fish are caught over continental shelves.

Great white sharks hunt fish and other animals over continental shelves.

Deep peaks

There are underwater mountains, known as seamounts, in all oceans. Great Meteor Seamount in the Atlantic is over 100km wide at its base and 4km high.

Mount Everest

Great Meteor Seamount

INTERNET LINKS

For links to websites about the undersea landscape, go to **www.usborne-quicklinks.com**

Rolling plains

The flattest places on Earth are the stretches of deep seabed called abyssal plains. They cover nearly half the sea floor. You could walk on them around the globe without climbing any more than 2m.

The tallest mountain on Earth is not Mount Everest, but Mauna Kea in the Pacific Ocean. This volcano rises 10,203m from the sea floor to form one of the Hawaiian islands. Everest is over 1,000m lower.

Everest

Sea level

Mauna Kea

Under pressure

The deeper you go under the sea, the greater the pressure of water pushing down on you. In the deepest ocean, the pressure on you would be equivalent to the weight of an elephant balanced on a stamp.

This is a submersible. It can withstand huge pressures to take explorers safely into the deep ocean.

Earth's deepest point is the 11,022m deep Mariana Trench in the Pacific. If a 1kg weight fell into the trench, it would take over an hour to reach the bottom.

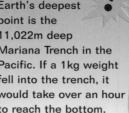

Avalanche

Seaquakes* can trigger avalanches of mud and sand which cascade down the continental slope. They can cover areas of the seabed the size of France with a layer of mud over 1m thick.

Deep sea carpet

About three quarters of the deep ocean floor is covered in a smooth ooze, mostly around 300m thick. It is made up of the dead bodies of animals and plants which drifted down and mixed with mud. The ooze layer grows just 6m every million years.

The remains of tiny shelled sea creatures, like these, sink slowly to the ocean floor.

Ocean	Average depth	Deepest point
Pacific Ocean	4,200m	11,022m
Atlantic Ocean	3,300m	9,560m
Indian Ocean	3,900m	9,000m
Southern Ocean	3,730m	8,264m
Arctic Ocean	1,300m	5,450m

Cold and dark

21°C—	
10°C—	
500m 4°C—	
3°C—	
1000m	
2.5°C—	
2°C—	
1500m	

The sea gets darker and colder the deeper you go. Most sunlight is absorbed in the top 10m of water. No light at all reaches below 1,000m, even on the sunniest day.

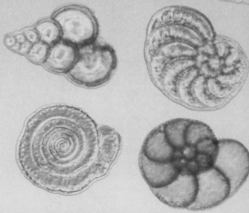

* See page 73

Oceans in Motion

The wind drives huge bands of water, called currents, around the world. The Antarctic circumpolar current flows around Antarctica. It carries over 2,000 times more water than Earth's largest river, the Amazon.

The world's main currents

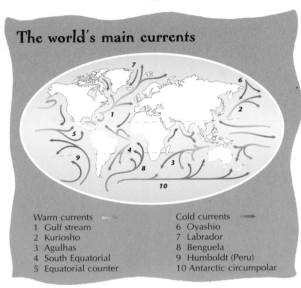

Warm currents
1 Gulf stream
2 Kuriosho
3 Agulhas
4 South Equatorial
5 Equatorial counter

Cold currents
6 Oyashio
7 Labrador
8 Benguela
9 Humboldt (Peru)
10 Antarctic circumpolar

Welling up

Near Peru, the cold Humboldt current raises minerals from the deep, feeding tiny sea plants. These in turn are food for millions of fish. In one year, 10 million tonnes of anchovies may be caught.

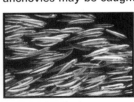

A school of anchovies

The ground under our feet rises and falls twice a day, just like the ocean tides. When the Moon is directly overhead, it rises by half a metre.

Timely tides

Twice a day, tides make the sea level rise and fall. Tides are caused by the Moon and Sun's gravity pulling water into giant bulges on the Earth.

Spring tide

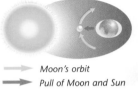

Moon's orbit
Pull of Moon and Sun

When the Moon and Sun pull in a straight line, they cause very high and very low tides. These are called spring tides.

Neap tide

Moon's orbit
Pull of Moon

When the Moon and Sun pull at right angles, the tides are more even. These are "neap tides". Spring and neap tides occur twice monthly.

Extreme tides

The greatest tides occur in the Bay of Fundy, Canada. They can rise high enough to cover a 5 storey building.

Tsunami terrors

Tsunamis are giant waves caused by earthquakes or undersea eruptions. They move as fast as jet planes. As they near land they rear up to great heights and can drown whole islands.

Undersea eruptions shake the seabed, causing the sea to form long, low tsunami waves.

If tsunamis reach the coast, they are squeezed up into huge waves that can cause disaster.

Making waves

Waves are caused by wind blowing over the sea. The stronger the wind and the longer it blows, the bigger the waves. Waves only break the water's surface.

Submarines only need to dive 100m to avoid even the harshest storms.

Junk that washes up on beaches is used to study how winds and currents work. In 1992, a ship spilled a cargo of rubber ducks in the Pacific. Scientists tracked their progress. Many were found in Alaska, but others are still going!

INTERNET LINKS
To find links to websites about waves and ocean currents, go to
www.usborne-quicklinks.com

Giant waves

The highest recorded natural wave was seen in the Pacific Ocean in 1933. It measured 34m – the height of a 10 storey building.

A wave is energy from the wind moving through water.

77

Along the Shore

Coast to coast

The combined length of all coastlines would reach to the Moon and halfway back. These are the top ten coastlines:

Country	Length
Canada	93,711km
Indonesia	54,716km
Greenland	44,087km
Russia	37,653km
Philippines	36,289km
Australia	25,760km
USA	19,924km
New Zealand	15,134km
China	14,500km
Greece	13,676km

Prickly character

Most sea urchins are fist-sized, but some grow to 36cm across. Using their spines and sharp teeth, sea urchins burrow into sand and rock. Over 20 years, one Californian sea urchin drilled 1cm into a solid steel girder.

Slimy seaweed

A danger faced by life on the shore is drying up when the tide goes out. Seaweeds keep moist by covering themselves with slimy mucus. The world's longest seaweed is the Pacific giant kelp. It grows over 50m long.

Giant kelp grows very quickly: up to 60cm a day.

Taking a beating

The coastline is constantly being worn away by the waves. This is called erosion. The waves carve out cliffs, caves and arches along the shore.

This rock arch off the coast of Oregon, USA, was carved out by the sea.

Purple sea urchins – very prickly

The highest sea cliffs in the world are on the north coast of Molokai, Hawaii. They are over a kilometre high.

The sea cliffs of Molokai are over three times as tall as the Eiffel Tower in France.

Sticky customer

Animals living on the shoreline have to survive being battered by the waves. A limpet clings to its rocky perch so firmly that it would take a force 2,000 times its own weight to prise it off.

Limpets live on algae, which they scrape from the rocks with a rasping tongue.

Mangroves

Mangrove trees grow in huge swamps where tropical rivers flow into the sea. The trees may be 40m tall. Salt water can kill plants so mangroves eject waste salt through their leaves or store it in old leaves which they then shed.

The mangroves' long, tangled roots anchor them in the mud.

Mudskippers are odd fish that spend much of their time out of the water in mangrove swamps. They breathe through their skin.

Mudskippers flip themselves along with their tails. They can leap over half a metre.

Hitching a lift

Hermit crabs borrow discarded seashells to house their soft bodies. As they grow, they find a bigger shell to live in.

A hermit crab in a borrowed shell

Seashore molluscs

Molluscs are a huge group of animals found on land and in water. They range from squid and octopuses to tiny seashells. These are some of the molluscs found along the shore:

Bivalves (Double shell)	Univalves (Single shell)
Mussel	Limpet
Oyster	Winkle
Scallop	Whelk
Razor shell	Cowrie

Sand colours

Sand forms when wind and rain wear down rocks into tiny pieces. Yellow sand contains tiny pieces of quartz. Pink or white sand contains coral, and black sand contains volcanic rock or coal. Rare green sand contains the mineral olivine.

INTERNET LINKS
For a link to a website where you can see a kelp forest with a live webcam, and more, go to **www.usborne-quicklinks.com**

Coral Reefs

Coral reefs are built by tiny animals called polyps. They use minerals in sea water to build skeletons around themselves. Polyps live in vast colonies. After death, they leave layers of hard limestone skeleton.

Most reef-building coral is very sensitive. It grows best in water with these features:

1. Temperature	Warm: 25-29°C	
2. Depth	Less than 25m deep	
3. Saltiness	No saltier than 30-40 parts per thousand	
4. Purity	Must be clear and unpolluted	

Every day, coral grows a new skeleton layer. The way it grows is affected by the seasons. Scientists studying fossil coral think that 400 million years ago a year was 400 days long. Days have shortened by three quarters of a second every century.

Skeleton of the mushroom coral

Coral islands

The Pacific has thousands of coral islands, called atolls. Thousands of years ago, they were coral reefs around volcanic islands. The volcano sank, but the coral kept growing to form a low-lying atoll around a shallow lagoon.

30 million BC
Volcano fringed with coral

Today
Coral atoll with lagoon

Some like it cold

Some of the world's largest coral reefs are actually found in the deep, cold waters of the North Atlantic. Off Scotland are hundreds of odd, coral-covered mounds called the Darwin Mounds. They are home to giant one-celled animals called xenophyophores, which can be over 20cm wide.

Coral reefs are home to thousands of animal species.

Home, sweet home

Pencil-thin pearlfish live in the bodies of sea cucumbers. Up to three spend the day sleeping inside one sea cucumber, their heads sticking out of its tail end.

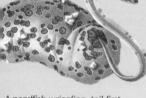

A pearlfish wriggling, tail first, into the body of a sea cucumber

Clamming up

The giant clam has the largest shell in the world. It can be 1.2m wide, and weigh over a quarter of a tonne. The two halves of the shell fit together so tightly that they can grip a thin wire.

Good shot

Pistol shrimps are just 5cm long but have deadly weapons. When hunting fish, the shrimp snaps its large right claw, making a sound like a pistol shot. This sends shockwaves through the water, stunning the fish. The shrimp then has time to close in for the kill.

Small cleaner wrasse run beauty parlours on the reef. Larger fish queue to have dead skin and parasites picked off their bodies. Even fierce moray eels sit still as their teeth are cleaned.

Cleaner wrasse at work

Longest reef

The longest coral reef is the Great Barrier Reef. It stretches over 2,000km off the coast of Queensland, Australia. It is the biggest structure ever formed by a living thing – it can even be seen from the Moon.

The Great Barrier Reef is shown in pink below.

Australia

Thorny problem

The Great Barrier Reef is being eaten away by crown of thorns starfish. To digest the coral, they push their stomachs out of their bodies to cover it. 15 starfish can eat an area of reef as big as a soccer pitch in 2½ years.

Crown of thorns starfish

INTERNET LINKS

To find links to websites about coral reefs, and the animals that live in them, go to **www.usborne-quicklinks.com**

Giant clam

Small Fry

Billions of tiny plants, called phytoplankton (meaning "drifting plants"), float near the sea surface. They use sunlight, and minerals from the water, to make their own food.

Without phytoplankton, little could live in the sea. They are eaten by small sea animals (zooplankton) which in turn are eaten by fish. Over two million million tonnes of phytoplankton grow each year.

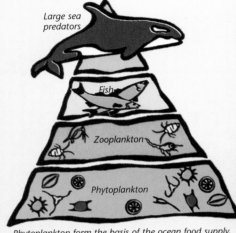

Large sea predators

Fish

Zooplankton

Phytoplankton

Phytoplankton form the basis of the ocean food supply.

The world's tiniest crabs have shells less than 6.5mm long. They are called pea crabs. They live and feed inside the shells of oysters, scallops and mussels.

Pea crab in a mussel shell

Titchy tiddlers

The smallest known sea fish is the dwarf goby from the Indian Ocean. Adults are only about 9mm long and could easily fit on a fingernail. Another dwarf goby, from Samoa, is the world's lightest fish. It would take 500 of them to weigh just 1g.

Part-time plankton

Sea slugs start life as tiny zooplankton with shells, floating near the sea surface. They grow up without having to compete with adults for food and space. Later they turn into adults without shells, such as the one below.

This extraordinary creature is an adult sea slug. This type grows 25mm long.

Short shark

The world's smallest shark is the spined pygmy shark from the Pacific Ocean. Adults measure just 15cm long. This is 120 times shorter than the whale shark, the world's largest shark.

Spined pygmy shark (a quarter life size)

! The main diet of the huge blue whale is a tiny, shrimp-like animal called krill. Krill are just 6cm long, but live in vast shoals. A blue whale sieves four tonnes of krill from the sea daily.

Shoals of krill can be several kilometres in length.

Blowing bubbles

The janthina snail lives at the sea surface. To stay afloat it blows bubbles, joining them together to make a raft from which it hangs upside down.

Red alert

In spring, many types of phytoplankton breed quickly in the warm weather. If those called dinoflagellates are involved, this can cause disaster. They are very poisonous. They turn the sea blood-red, with as many as 6,000 of them in one drop of water. They kill millions of fish and shellfish.

Dinoflagellates – tiny but deadly

INTERNET LINKS

To find links to websites about small sea creatures, go to **www.usborne-quicklinks.com**

Seahorse slowcoach

Seahorses are the slowest fish. They hover in the water, powered by their tiny back fins. Even at top speed, it would take a seahorse 2½ days to travel 1km. Dwarf seahorses live in the Gulf Stream current, south of Bermuda. They are just 40mm long.

Dwarf seahorse (three times life size)

Smallest fry	Group	Average size
Ammonicera rota	Shells	0.5mm long
Sea biscuit	Sea urchin	5.5mm wide
Cushion star	Starfish	9mm wide
Parateuthis tunicata	Squid	12.7mm long
Octopus arborescens	Octopus	50mm wide
Cape lobster	Lobster	10cm long
Kemps ridley	Turtle	70cm long

Life in the Depths

Deep in the oceans, the water is pitch black and very cold. Despite this, thousands of fish and invertebrates live there.

Lantern fish light up the deep.

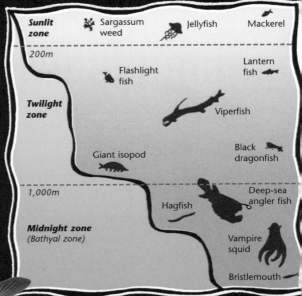

Sunlit zone	Sargassum weed	Jellyfish	Mackerel

200m

Flashlight fish

Lantern fish

Twilight zone

Viperfish

Giant isopod

Black dragonfish

1,000m

Deep-sea angler fish

Hagfish

Midnight zone (Bathyal zone)

Vampire squid

Bristlemouth

Flashlight fish

Many deep-sea fish make their own lights. Flashlight fish have patches under their eyes which contain billions of glowing bacteria. If danger comes, they hide the lights with flaps of skin.

Flashlight fish with glowing eye patches

Many deep-sea prawns are bright red. Red is hard to see in deep water, and many deep-sea fish are colour-blind. One fish, the black dragonfish, has eyes that can see it. It also shines its own red light to hunt for the prawns.

Sticking together

Finding a mate is hard in the dark, so angler fish make sure they stay in touch. The male weighs half a million times less than the female. He grips her with his teeth and their bodies merge. All that is left of him is a pouch on her side which fertilizes her eggs.

Angling for food

An angler fish uses lights to trap food. A long, thin fin like a fishing rod grows over its head. It has a glowing bulb dangling on the end, which acts like bait. Small fish mistake it for a meal and swim straight into the angler's mouth.

The angler fish's lure is made up of tiny, glowing bacteria.

INTERNET LINKS
To find links to websites about the creatures of the deep go to
www.usborne-quicklinks.com

If attacked, the eel-like hagfish wraps itself in a cocoon of sticky slime. To leave the cocoon, it ties itself in a knot, then passes the knot down its body, wiping the slime away.

A hagfish getting knotted

Vicious viper

The viperfish is named for its long fangs and snake-like body. When hunting another sea animal, it swims rapidly forward, jaws open, and impales it on its front teeth. It also has lights inside its mouth which attract curious prey.

Viperfish have rows of hexagon-shaped lights along the sides of their bodies. These may be used to attract mates.

Roly poly monsters

Giant isopods live 1km down on the sea floor. These armour-plated invertebrates are related to the common pill bug. When threatened, they roll up into a ball just like their land-dwelling relatives.

Giant isopods grow half a metre long.

Undersea lake

Scientists exploring 900m down in the Gulf of Mexico made an amazing discovery: a lake. Called a brine pool, its water is much saltier, and so heavier, than the sea water above. Its shores are surrounded by thousands of mussels which are able to make energy from methane gas seeping from the pool. This means they can live without sunlight.

These mussels live as near to the brine pool as they can – but if they fall in, they die.

The viperfish's teeth are so long that they do not all fit inside its mouth.

Animal	Greatest depth found
Prawn	6,373m
Sea urchin	7,340m
Sea spider	7,370m
Barnacle	7,880m
Fish (brotulid)	8,372m
Sponge	9,990m
Starfish	9,990m
Sea snail	10,687m
Sea anemone	10,730m
Sea cucumber	10,911m

Deeper Still

Over half the ocean floor lies below 4,000m, in the "abyssal zone". 6,000m down, trenches* plunge deeper still. This is the "hadal zone", named after Hades, the ancient Greek world of the dead; yet it is far from dead – millions of animals live there.

Tripod fish

Tripod fish have three very long fins. They use them like stilts to rest on the seafloor, while waiting for drifting food.

Tripod fish resting on the sea floor

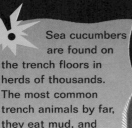

Sea cucumbers are found on the trench floors in herds of thousands. The most common trench animals by far, they eat mud, and filter out its nutrients.

Sea cucumber grazing

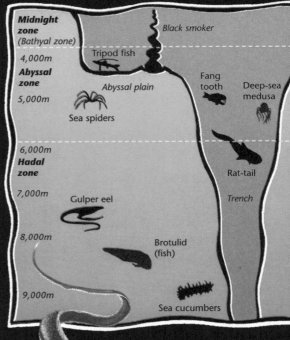

Midnight zone (Bathyal zone)

Black smoker

4,000m

Tripod fish

Abyssal zone

Abyssal plain

Fang tooth

Deep-sea medusa

5,000m

Sea spiders

6,000m

Hadal zone

7,000m

Gulper eel

Rat-tail

Trench

8,000m

Brotulid (fish)

9,000m

Sea cucumbers

Big mouth

Gulper eels feed on dead animals drifting down from the surface. A tiny shrimp may take a week to fall 3km, so the eels make the most of any food they find. They have huge mouths and stretchy stomachs for swallowing prey larger than themselves.

Gulper eels swim onto their prey with their enormous mouths gaping wide.

*See Sliding under, page 72

Deep drummer

Rat-tails are one of the commonest deep-sea fish. Males are believed to attract mates in the dark depths by making a drumming noise with muscles inside their bodies.

Rat-tails can grow over a metre in length.

Sea spiders

Sea spiders are distant cousins of land spiders. They stride around the sea floor on their long legs, feeding on anemones with their tube-like mouths.

Sea spiders are found in most seas.

Deep sea problem	Adaptation	Example
Food is scarce	Grow more slowly Big mouth to catch food	Deep-sea clam Gulper eel
No light	Make own lights Developed sense of smell Super-developed eyes Movement-sensing organs	Lantern fish Angler fish Squid Brotulid (fish)

Black smokers

In some parts of the ocean where new seafloor is forming*, there are openings, called vents, which pour out super-hot water. Minerals from the rock build up around the vents into chimney stacks as tall as houses. Mineral-rich water gushes out of them.

Minerals in vent water turn it as dark as smoke.

INTERNET LINKS
To find links to websites about deep ocean vents, and the animals that live around them, go to **www.usborne-quicklinks.com**

A colony of giant tube worms

Animals survive in deep Pacific vents where the water is full of toxic chemicals and over 300°C. Giant tube worms grow up to 2m long. Their bodies contain bacteria that make energy from the chemicals.

*See *Seafloor spread*, page 73

Attack and Defence

The great white shark has huge jaws filled with rows of triangular, razor-sharp teeth. Each tooth may be over 7cm long. As the front teeth wear out, the next row moves forward to replace them. Odd objects have been found in sharks' stomachs, including coats, a full bottle of wine and a porcupine.

Great white shark

Super smell

Sharks can smell blood from injured prey nearly 500m away. The nostrils of a hammerhead shark are at the ends of its hammer-shaped head. If it smells food, it swings its head from side to side to find the way to it.

The hammerhead shark – named for obvious reasons

Electric shock

Some fish use electric shocks to kill prey and defend themselves. The most powerful electric sea fish is the black torpedo ray. It makes enough electricity to power a television set.

Black torpedo ray

Deadly tentacles

The Portuguese man-of-war stuns prey with its long, stinging tentacles. These trail over 30m from its floating body. Once they have trapped some food, the tentacles can shrink quickly to 15cm long, so that it can be passed to the mouth.

Portuguese man-of-war

A starfish can escape its attackers by leaving some arms behind. All starfish can grow new arms, but some can grow a whole new body from just a tiny piece of arm.

Starfish may look odd while they are regrowing limbs.

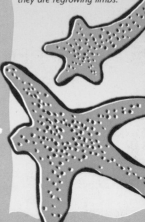

Sinister stones

Stonefish have double protection. They are well camouflaged on the sea floor, looking just like weed-covered rocks. They also have poisonous spines, which can pierce a diver's rubber shoe.

Can you spot the stonefish?

Poison platter

Parts of the death puffer fish are highly poisonous, and can kill a person in two hours. It is eaten in Japan, but chefs must train for three years before serving it. People still die from eating it.

INTERNET LINKS
To find links to websites about ocean predators and prey, go to **www.usborne-quicklinks.com**

Smokescreen

Cuttlefish squirt out thick clouds of brown ink to confuse their enemies. This gives the cuttlefish time to escape. Cuttlefish ink is called sepia, and was once used as artists' ink and in photography.

Cuttlefish can change colour to match their surroundings.

A sea cucumber has a striking way of foiling enemies. If one comes too close, it entangles it with sticky, spaghetti-like threads, enabling the cucumber to flee.

A sea cucumber fending off a crab

Hired defences

Spanish shawl sea slugs combine self-defence with a good meal. They eat sea anemones, complete with their stinging cells. The cells travel through the slug's body and rest just under its skin. If the sea slug is touched, the borrowed stinging cells shoot into its enemy.

Spanish shawl sea slug

Sailing by

The sailfish can swim at 109kph – faster than the cheetah, the fastest land animal. At high speed, the fish's sail-like back fin folds down into a groove, and its other fins press close to its body.

Sailfish cruising...

Sailfish at full throttle

Fish	Top speed
Sailfish	109kph
Bluefin tuna	100kph
Swordfish	90kph
Marlin	80kph
Wahoo	77kph
Yellowfin tuna	74kph
Blue shark	69kph
Flying fish	56kph
Barracuda	43kph
Mackerel	33kph

Sea Mammals

Until about 65 million years ago, the ancestors of whales and dolphins lived on land. Here are some of the ways they later adapted to water:

Pakicetus, the earliest known whale, probably spent most of its time on land.

- Bodies became streamlined for swimming.
- Front legs became flippers.
- Back legs disappeared altogether.
- Nostrils became a blowhole on the top of the head.
- Hair was replaced by a thick, warm layer of fat, called blubber, under the skin.

Record breaking blues

The blue whale is the largest sea mammal, and the biggest animal ever. An adult can weigh up to 190 tonnes – as much as 50 rhinos. Its tongue alone weighs three tonnes, heavier than 35 men.

Mammal group	Members
Cetaceans	Whales; dolphins; porpoises
Pinnipeds	Seals; sealions; walruses
Sirenians	Manatees; dugongs

A newborn blue whale can weigh over five tonnes – a thousand times heavier than a newborn human. By the age of seven months, it weighs as much as two buses.

The biggest whale on record was 33m long.

A baby blue whale drinks 600 litres of its mother's milk a day.

Sperm whales can hold their breath for two hours. One was found with two deep-sea sharks in its stomach. It must have dived 3,000m to catch them.

Bubble trouble

A humpback whale can trap its food by blowing bubbles. It circles a shoal of fish and blows a big net of bubbles around them. This confuses and traps the fish. The whale then swims up, mouth open, gulping the fish down.

Humpback whale

Mammal	Diet	Daily amount
Blue whale	Krill, shrimps	4 tonnes
Sperm whale	Squid, sharks	1 tonne
Elephant seal	Squid, fish	200kg
Orca (killer whale)	Seals, birds, sharks	45kg
Bottlenose dolphin	Fish, eels, hermit crabs	8-15kg

Dolphin detective

Dolphins use sound to navigate underwater. They give out clicks much higher than humans can hear. If the sounds hit objects in the water, they send back echoes. From these, the dolphin can tell where and what an object is.

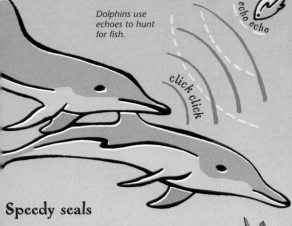

Dolphins use echoes to hunt for fish.

echo echo

click click

Speedy seals

Seals, sealions and walruses belong to a group of sea mammals called pinnipeds. The fastest pinniped is the Californian sealion. It can speed through the water at 40kph. Leopard seals also swim quickly when hunting penguins. To land, they rocket out of the water and crash onto the ice.

INTERNET LINKS
To find links to websites about mammals that live in the sea, go to **www.usborne-quicklinks.com**

Californian sealions are amazing acrobats.

A walrus has about 700 whiskers on its snout. It uses them to find shellfish under the sea. The whiskers are so thick, Inuit people use them as toothpicks.

A walrus's whiskers are 40 times thicker than a cat's.

Actual size

Sea elephant

The biggest pinniped is the huge Southern elephant seal. The largest on record was 6.5m long and weighed 4 tonnes. If it reared up, it would have towered up to 3m in height.

Southern elephant seals

Mermaid myth

Some say that manatees started the mermaid legend. When Christopher Columbus first saw one, he wrote that mermaids were not as beautiful as he had heard.

Manatee.... or mermaid?

Ocean Giants

The whale shark is the world's biggest fish. It grows over 18m long and weighs 20 tonnes – as much as five rhinos. It also has the thickest skin of any animal: it is like tough rubber, 10cm thick. Despite its size, this huge fish eats only plankton.

Whale sharks suck in huge amounts of water, sieve out the plankton, then blow the water out through gill slits (openings for breathing)

The gill slits are in this area.

The Arctic lion's mane jellyfish has a mane of tentacles which can trail for over 36m – longer than a blue whale. It is the world's largest jellyfish.

Arctic lion's mane jellyfish

King crab

Crabs, lobsters and shrimps belong to a group of animals called crustaceans. Japanese spider crabs are the largest crustaceans known. The biggest spider crab ever found measured 3.7m across its front claws.

Spider crabs are named for their long, spindly legs.

Manta rays have special fins for feeding.

Mighty manta

Diamond-shaped manta rays are the largest type of ray. They can weigh over two tonnes and have an 8m "wingspan". Rays swim through the water by flapping their wings. They can also leap 2m out of the water.

INTERNET LINKS
To find links to websites about the giants that live in the ocean, go to **www.usborne-quicklinks.com**

Awesome oarfish

Sharks and rays have skeletons of gristly cartilage. Other fish have bony skeletons. The longest bony fish is the oarfish. It can grow over 15m in length: longer than a bus.

Prize pearl

Sometimes, clams and oysters get irritating parasites or sand grains in their shells. They coat them with layers of calcium carbonate, forming pearls. The biggest pearl, the 6.4kg Pearl of Lao-Tzu, came from a giant clam.

Natural pearls, like the one in this oyster, are very rare. Just one is found in every 10,000 shells.

Ocean giant	Group	Biggest ever
Giant Pacific octopus	Octopus	4m long
Pacific leatherback	Turtle	2.54m long
Midgardia xandaros	Starfish	1.38m wide
Loggerhead sponge	Sponge	1.05m tall
Trumpet conch	Snail	0.77m long
Discoma	Sea anemone	0.61m wide
Giant clam	Bivalve	333kg
American lobster	Lobster	20kg

Squids in

The giant squid is one of the largest known invertebrates. The biggest giant squid on record washed up in Thimble Tickle Bay, Canada, in 1878. It was 17m long and weighed over two tonnes. Huge as they are, scientists have never seen an adult alive in its natural surroundings.

The eyes of giant squid are the size of basketballs: the biggest of any animal.

Ocean sunfish start life as a tiny egg the size of a pinhead, yet an adult is the size of a small truck: over 3m long, and weighing over 2 tonnes. The ocean sunfish is the heaviest bony fish.

The favourite food of the ocean sunfish is the moon jellyfish.

Birds of the Sea

There are about 300 sea bird species. They are divided into three groups (see right), depending on where they find their food.

Coast birds
cormorant; pelican; gull

Offshore birds
diving petrel; penguin; puffin; frigate bird; tern; gannet; guillemot

Open ocean birds
albatross; fulmar; petrel; kittiwake; shearwater; skua

Frigate express

The magnificent frigate bird is the fastest sea bird. It can fly at over 150kph. On some South Sea islands, people have trained frigate birds to carry messages between islands.

Salt surplus

Sea birds take in lots of salt water as they feed. Too much salt kills birds, so special glands in their heads remove salt from the water. It trickles out of the birds' nostrils.

Sea birds lose salt through their nostrils.

Skuas and gulls have built-in sunglasses. Their eyes contain drops of reddish oil, which block out the harsh sunlight and the glare reflected from the sea.

About tern

Many sea birds travel far between their feeding and breeding grounds. Each year the Arctic tern flies from the Arctic to the Antarctic and back again, a round trip of over 40,000km. Arctic terns start to fly south when they are just two or three months old.

In its lifetime, an Arctic tern flies the same distance as a return trip to the Moon.

Head over heels

Sea eagles perform highly unusual courtship displays. The male dives down towards the female, and the two birds lock their talons together. They then plummet downwards, turning cartwheels in mid-air.

Sea eagles tumble through the air when courting.

Sea wanderer

The wandering albatross has the longest wingspan of any living bird – up to 3.5m. It glides on air currents across the Southern Ocean. If the winds are right, an albatross can fly 1,000km in a day.

Albatrosses are very efficient gliders, conserving energy as they soar.

Guillemots live in colonies of over 14,000 birds. They lay their eggs on narrow cliff ledges. The eggs are long and have pointed ends: ideally adapted not to fall off. If they are knocked, they just roll in a circle.

Guillemot eggs roll around, but not away.

Baby sitting

Emperor penguins nest on the Antarctic ice in midwinter, enduring temperatures of –62°C. The female lays one egg, then swims off. The male stays to tend the egg. He balances it on his feet and spends about nine weeks without moving or eating. The female returns to feed the chick when it hatches.

INTERNET LINKS
To find links to websites about sea birds, fly along to
www.usborne-quicklinks.com

Spitting with rage

To drive intruders away from their nests, fulmars spit at them. Fulmars eat plankton, which makes the spit oily and smelly. They can hit targets up to a metre away very accurately.

Penguins have special flaps to keep eggs and chicks warm.

Fulmars live in and around cold seas.

Walking on water

Wilson's storm petrel is one of the smallest sea birds. As it flutters above the sea looking for plankton to eat, it pats the water's surface with its feet. This makes it seem to be walking on the water.

Wilson's storm petrel is the most common sea bird.

Penguin facts

Largest	Emperor penguin	Up to 120cm tall
Smallest	Little blue penguin	40cm tall
Fastest swimmer	Gentoo penguin	Up to 40kph
Deepest diver	Emperor penguin	Record of 518m
Most common	Macaroni penguin	Over 20 million
Rarest	Yellow-eyed penguin	11,000
Most northerly	Galápagos penguin	From Galápagos Islands

The Pacific Ocean

The Pacific is the largest ocean, covering about a third of the Earth. At its widest point, between Panama and Malaysia, it stretches nearly halfway round the world.

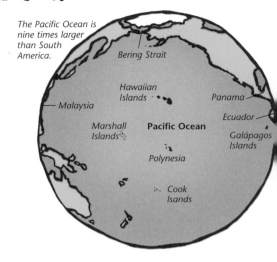

The Pacific Ocean is nine times larger than South America.

Bering Strait
Hawaiian Islands
Malaysia
Panama
Ecuador
Marshall Islands
Pacific Ocean
Galápagos Islands
Polynesia
Cook Isands

Vital statistics

Area	155,557,000km²
Widest point	17,700km
Narrowest point	11,000km
Average depth	4,200m
Greatest depth	11,022m

Land bridge

The Pacific's narrowest part is the Bering Strait, which divides the USA and Russia by 85km. 14,000 years ago, the sea level was lower, and the Strait was dry land. The first people to live in North America crossed over this land bridge.

Sea serpents

There are about 50 species of Pacific sea snake, ranging from 1-3m in length. All use poison to kill fish for food. One drop of sea snake venom could kill three people.

Sea snakes are the most poisonous of all snakes.

Epic voyages

Pacific island sailors were the first to explore the Pacific, over 2,000 years ago. They were experts at navigating by the wind, waves, Sun and stars.

Marshall Islanders used stick chart like this, to map currents around their islands (marked by shells).

! Grey whales swim 20,000km each year. They spend the summer feeding in the Arctic. They then swim south along the Pacific coast to breed near Mexico, returning north in the spring.

Grey whales' bodies are often covered with barnacles.

Mountain maker

Along Chile's coast, the undersea plate that forms the Pacific floor meets the South American plate. This causes the continent to buckle upwards as the Pacific plate dives beneath it*. This process formed the Andes mountains about 80 million years ago, and they are still growing.

The Pacific floor sinks under the continent of South America.

South America buckles, and the Andes grow.

Sea dreams

Sea otters live on the Pacific coast of North America, in beds of giant kelp**. They spend most of their lives at sea, even sleeping in the water.

Sea otters wind strands of kelp around their bodies to stop them drifting away as they sleep.

Giant Galápagos tortoises can live for 200 years – longer than all other land animals. They live in the Galápagos Islands, west of Ecuador. These are also home to rare marine iguanas, the only lizards that live mainly in the sea.

Giant Galápagos tortoise

Tropical islands

The Pacific is dotted with islands. Over 100 ancient volcanoes make up the Hawaiian islands – a chain 2,800km long. Hawaii itself is made up of two huge volcanoes – Mauna Loa and Mauna Kea.

INTERNET LINKS

To find links to websites with more information on the Pacific Ocean, go to **www.usborne-quicklinks.com**

This beautiful lagoon is in the Cook Islands.

*See *Sliding under*, page 72; **See *Slimy seaweed*, page 78

The Atlantic Ocean

Vital statistics

Area	76,762,000km²
Widest part	4,830km
Narrowest part	2,848km
Average depth	3,300m
Greatest depth	9,560m

Still growing

The Atlantic is the second largest ocean, covering a fifth of the Earth. Each year, it grows about 4cm wider, pushing Europe and North America apart. When Columbus crossed the Atlantic in 1492, it was 20m narrower than it is today.

Columbus's flagship, the Santa Maria

Mid-Atlantic Ridge

The longest mountain range in the world, the Mid-Atlantic Ridge, runs down the middle of the Atlantic Ocean. The mountains are up to 4km high, but their tips are still 2.5km under the surface of the sea.

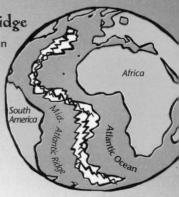

The Mid-Atlantic Ridge is over 11,000km long.

INTERNET LINKS

To find links to websites about the Atlantic Ocean, its wildlife, and hurricanes go to **www.usborne-quicklinks.com**

Two South Atlantic islands are record-breakingly remote. Bouvet Island is the most isolated island. It is 1,600km away from Africa. The remotest inhabited island is Tristan da Cunha, 1,500km from Africa.

Hurricanes

Many hurricanes begin in the Atlantic. They form a warm air rises over the equator. This causes low pressure, which sucks the winds into a whirling cloud. In 1992, Hurricane Andrew hit Florida, making more than a million people homeless.

The spiralling winds of a hurricane, seen here, can reach speeds of over 200kph.

Wreckage caused by a hurricane.

Turtle tour

Atlantic green turtles leave their feeding grounds in Brazil and swim 2,000km to lay their eggs on Ascension Island in the middle of the Atlantic. Scientists believe they find their way with an in-built magnetic compass.

Atlantic green turtles swim halfway across the Atlantic to lay their eggs.

Spouting off

Waterspouts are common in the Gulf of Mexico. They form when tornadoes pass from land to sea. Winds blowing up to 965kph whip the sea into clouds of spray. Waterspouts can be 120m high.

A waterspout off the Florida coast

Unsalty sea

For 180km off the coast of Brazil, the Atlantic is hardly salty at all. This is due to the huge amount of water poured into it by the Amazon River. The Amazon carries over half the fresh water on earth.

Still waters

The Sargasso Sea in the North Atlantic is an area of calm water larger than India. Huge rafts of seaweed float on its surface, sheltering some unique animals. The Sargassum fish is camouflaged to look like seaweed.

Can you see the Sargassum fish hiding in the seaweed?

Each year, eels swim from rivers in Europe to breed in the Sargasso Sea. The adults then die, and the young eels begin an amazing return journey. They are only 8cm long, but they swim 6,000km in about three years.

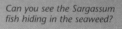

Young eel (half life size)

Lobster conga

Each year, thousands of spiny lobsters migrate over 100km along Florida's Atlantic coast. Troops of about 50 lobsters march in single file, as fast as a human can swim, hooking their claws round the lobster in front.

Spiny lobster

The Indian Ocean

Vital statistics

Area	73,600,000km²
Widest part	10,000km
Average depth	3,900m
Greatest depth	9,000m
Volume	292,131,000km³

Warm 'n' salty

The Indian Ocean is the third largest ocean. It is also the warmest and saltiest. The surface temperature in the Persian Gulf can reach 35.6°C in summer. The Red Sea is the saltiest sea in the world*.

Flying fish

To escape enemies, flying fish shoot out of the water at speeds of over 30kph. They then glide over the surface using their tails as propellers and fins as wings. After about 40m, they bounce on the surface to give them extra lift. They can glide for up to 400m.

Flying fish can glide twice as fast as they swim.

Flying fish are found in the Indian Ocean.

Killer cone

The Indian Ocean is home to the most dangerous snail in the world: the cone shell. Inside its shell it has a trunk-like tube, full of deadly poison, which it injects into its prey.

Flying fish take off from the sea by rapidly flapping their tails.

At night, the surface of the Indian Ocean sparkles with light made by tiny plants called dinoflagellates**. Large numbers of them give off enough light to read by.

Cone shell feeding on a small cowrie

Pearly nautilus

The pearly nautilus lives in the Indian Ocean. Its shell is split into 40 chambers. It lives in the largest one. By altering the amount of gas in the chambers, the nautilus makes itself either float or sink.

Nautilus shell

*The Dead Sea is saltier, but is counted as a lake; **See *Red alert*, page 83

In 1938, scientists caught an odd fish near Madagascar. They were amazed to find it was a coelacanth, thought to be extinct for millions of years. They found that locals often caught them, and used their rough scales as sandpaper!

Coelacanth – not extinct after all.

Flashy fish

Many Indian Ocean fish have bright colours. This helps them to hide in the colourful reefs, and tells predators that they might be poisonous.

Blue moon angelfish

Golden butterfly fish

INTERNET LINKS
To find links to Indian Ocean websites, go to **www.usborne-quicklinks.com**

Deep sea fan

Sediment (mud and rocks) from the Indus and Ganges rivers pours into the Indian Ocean. It sinks to the bottom to form layers hundreds of metres thick. Undersea avalanches carry the sediment downwards, where it fans out, forming the "Bengal Fan". It stretches halfway across the Indian Ocean.

Alternating current

Most currents flow in one direction all the time. In the northern Indian Ocean, though, monsoon winds cause them to alter their direction twice a year. From October to April the currents are blown towards Africa. In May the currents flow towards India.

May-October:
October-April:

Big bang

In 1883, a huge eruption blew up two thirds of the island of Krakatoa in the Indian Ocean. The sound was the loudest ever recorded. It was heard over 4,800km away in Australia.

The shockwaves caused a huge tsunami to sweep over Java and Sumatra. It killed 36,000 people, and carried boats 3km inland.

These are the remains of Krakatoa, which blew up in 1883.

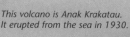

A map showing the spread of the Bengal Fan in the Indian Ocean

This volcano is Anak Krakatau. It erupted from the sea in 1930.

The Arctic Ocean

The Arctic Ocean is the smallest and shallowest ocean. It is almost entirely surrounded by land. It is frozen for most of the year, with the North Pole in the centre of a huge, floating raft of ice (the "ice cap"). In winter, the ice cap is up to 1.5km thick.

Canada
North Pole
Arctic Ocean
Russia
Greenland

Vital statistics

Area	14,090,000km²
Area of ice	10,000,000km² (permanent) 14,090,000km² (winter)
Sea ice* thickness	3m (average)
Average depth	1,300m
Greatest depth	5,450m

Iced water

Fresh water freezes at 0°C, but sea water at -2°C because salt lowers the freezing point. Frozen sea water, though, contains very little salt, as only the water part freezes. It can be melted down to make drinking water.

Sea unicorns

Male narwhals in the Arctic Ocean have a special feature shared by no other whale. They have a tusk which extends from their upper lips. It is actually a tooth, and can grow 2.5m long.

In the Middle Ages, narwhal tusks were sold as unicorn horns.

Polar bears can stand 1½ times the height of a person (2.6m).

Drifting off

The Arctic gets its name from the Greek word *arktos*, meaning "bear". It is home to huge polar bears, which can weigh over a tonne. Some bears drift for hundreds of kilometres out to sea on ice rafts. Some never go on land in their lives.

Polar bears are the largest type of bear, yet a newborn cub is so tiny that its mother can hide it between her toes. A cub grows so fast, though, that in a year it is as big as an adult human.

Polar bear cubs stay with their mothers for at least 2 years.

*Sea ice: ice floating on the sea around the main ice cap

Midnight Sun

In June and July the North Pole has constant daylight. At the same time, the South Pole has 24 hour darkness. In December and January it is the South Pole's turn for the "midnight Sun" and the North Pole is freezing and dark.

Midsummer at the North Pole
The Earth's tilt gives the North Pole 24 hour sunshine.

Midwinter at the North Pole
The Earth's tilt keeps the North Pole in the dark.

Not all icebergs are white. They range in colour from pure white to blue, green or even black. The colour of icebergs is affected by their size, age and minerals in the ice.

Old icebergs are often blue.

Icebreakers

Icebreakers are ships used to break through thick sea ice. They have sloping bows which pull the ship up onto the ice ahead. The ship's weight then presses down and breaks a path through the ice.

An icebreaker moving through ice

Orca ahoy

Orcas, also called killer whales, are one of the Arctic Ocean's most fearsome predators, although they are not known to harm humans. They usually hunt in groups, and share their kills.

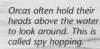

Orcas often hold their heads above the water to look around. This is called spy hopping.

Fire and ice

Deep under the Arctic Ocean is the Gakkel Ridge, a chain of volcanoes that runs for 1,500km. A rift running down the centre of the ridge contains vents*. Hot water gushing from the vents warms the ocean, and animals such as shrimp and sponges flourish there.

*See *Black smokers*, page 87

INTERNET LINKS
To find links to websites about the Arctic, and Arctic animals, go to
www.usborne-quicklinks.com

The Southern Ocean

The Southern Ocean is made up of the seas around Antarctica. In winter, an area of ocean twice the size of Canada is totally frozen over.

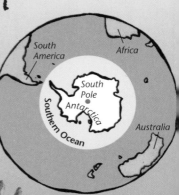

The Southern Ocean

Vital statistics

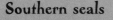

Area	35,000,000km²
Area of ice	4,000,000km² (permanent)
	21,000,000km² (in winter)
Sea ice thickness	0.75m (average)
Average depth	4,200m
Greatest depth	7,235m

Southern seals

The Weddell seal lives further south than any other mammal. It has to dive over 300m under the ice to find food. It can stay under for an hour, but must surface to breathe.

Weddell seals gnaw air holes in the ice with their big front teeth.

Millennium ocean

The boundary of the Southern Ocean was the last to be decided. In the year 2000, it was agreed worldwide that a circle of ocean ringing the continent of Antarctica would be known as the Southern Ocean. Its waters used to belong to the Atlantic, Pacific and Indian Oceans.

Round and round

The Southern Ocean flows clockwise around Antarctica. It is driven by the fast Antarctic circumpolar current. This is the largest of all currents, holding 100 times the water of all the world's rivers.

There are no penguins in the Arctic. They only live south of the equator. The four species found in Antarctica are well suited to the cold. Their feathers form windproof, waterproof coats so warm that the penguins can get too hot. They ruffle their feathers and extend their flippers to cool down.

Gentoo penguin

Some Antarctic cod have a chemical in their blood which acts as a natural antifreeze. It keeps their blood liquid even if the ocean temperature is several degrees below freezing.

Antarctic cod

Sky lights

In both the Arctic and the Antarctic, swirling light displays, called auroras, can be seen in the sky. They are caused by electrically charged particles in the atmosphere colliding with atoms of gas.

Ice mountains

The Southern and Arctic Oceans are littered with icebergs. These break off glaciers or ice sheets. The largest iceberg ever was seen off the Antarctic coast in 1956. Above water, its surface area was larger than Belgium.

Iced soup

Despite the cold, the Southern Ocean teems with life. In summer the water holds a huge amount of plankton which is eaten by small animals, such as krill. The krill are eaten in turn by birds, seals and whales. Krill form swarms so vast they can be seen from satellites.

Antarctic krill, half life-size

The aurora australis, also called the southern lights, glows above Antarctica.

INTERNET LINKS
To find links to websites about the Southern Ocean go to
www.usborne-quicklinks.com

The world's largest icebergs are found in the Southern Ocean.

Early Sea Explorers

From the 15th to the 18th centuries, many great explorers set out to discover new trade routes across the oceans. The map below shows some of the most famous voyages of that time.

- Christopher Columbus (1492-1493)
- Vasco da Gama (1497-1499)
- Ferdinand Magellan (1519-1522)
- Francis Drake (1577-1580)
- William Barents (1594-1596)
- James Cook (1768-1780)

! The first sea expedition in history was made by a North African called Hanno in 2750 BC. He sailed down the Red Sea to explore the coast of Africa, later returning with spices and treasure.

Early traders hoped to find rare spices. This is pepper growing in the wild.

Viking voyagers

The Vikings may have been the first Europeans to reach America. In about 986, Eric the Red voyaged to Greenland, and started a settlement there. Later, his son, Leif the Lucky, is thought to have sailed across the Atlantic to America.

The Vikings sailed 600km across the Atlantic in ships like this.

Chris's miss

Columbus is famous for reaching America, but he only found it by accident. He sailed west from Spain looking for a route to Asia. When he came to the Bahamas he thought he had found China. He never realized his mistake.

Studying the sea

HMS Challenger set out in 1872, from Portsmouth, England, on the first scientific voyage round the world. The expedition lasted for 3½ years, and its zig-zag route covered a distance of over 100,000km.

HMS Challenger's sealife laboratory

HMS Challenger was the first ship to sail all around the globe for science.

The achievements of *HMS Challenger*

- Measured the depth of the oceans, discovering, on the way, the deepest part of the Pacific, now named the Challenger Deep

- Discovered the Mid-Atlantic Ridge* – although many people at the time thought it was the fabled sunken continent of Atlantis

- Discovered over 4,000 new species of ocean animals and plants

- Discovered that life existed in the ocean's deepest, coldest depths

- The first in-depth study of ocean currents and temperatures

Monstrous maps

Hundreds of years ago, sea travel was perilous as many seas were uncharted. People imagined that all kinds of terrifying creatures lived in the oceans. Old maps are often illustrated with these monsters.

INTERNET LINKS
To find links to websites about early ocean explorers, and ocean scientists, go to **www.usborne-quicklinks.com**

*See page 98

Great ball of steel

In 1934, William Beebe and Otis Barton set an ocean depth record. They were lowered on a chain 923m into the ocean off Bermuda, in a large steel ball called a bathysphere. They reported what they saw through its tiny porthole, by telephone, back to those on the surface.

Beebe and Barton by their bathysphere in Bermuda

A map full of monsters

Modern Exploration

Jacques Cousteau and Émile Gagnan invented scuba* gear in 1943. Scuba gear is made up of cylinders of compressed air, a mouthpiece, and a "regulator", which feeds the diver just the right amount of air.

Scuba gear allows divers to work at depths of up to 70m.

INTERNET LINKS
To find links to websites about exploring the ocean today go to **www.usborne-quicklinks.com**

Sea floor maps

Scientists map deep-sea features, such as ridges, using echoes. Scientific instruments are towed above the seabed to chart areas 60km wide. Satellites are used to map sea depth by looking for changes in the Earth's gravity.

Satellite map of part of the North Atlantic Ocean

Record breakers

In 1958, the American nuclear submarine *Nautilus* crossed the Arctic Ocean beneath the ice, a distance of 2,945km. It was the first vessel to reach the North Pole. In 1960, the nuclear submarine *Triton* made the first underwater trip around the world.

Deep divers

Atmospheric diving suits (ADS) have built-in air supplies. They let divers work safely hundreds of metres below the sea.

A "Wasp" ADS has metal hands agile enough to do a jigsaw puzzle.

! Divers sometimes suffer from "the bends". Nitrogen gas in their air supplies dissolves in the blood. If divers rise too quickly, nitrogen bubbles form in their blood. This can cause sharp pains, or even death.

Diving record	Greatest depth	Year set	Holder
Holding breath	152m	2000	Loic Leferme (France)
Scuba (breathing air)	155m	1994	Daniel Manion (USA)
Scuba (breathing gas mixture)	308m	2001	John Bennett (UK)
Helmeted dive	534m	1988	Operation Comex Hydra 8 (France)
Submersible	10,978m	1995	*Kaiko* (Japan)

Alvin

Submersibles are small submarines used for deep-sea exploration. The submersible *Alvin* has mechanical arms, which are used to collect seabed samples, such as mud and rocks.

Scientists in Alvin discovered deep sea vents* in the Pacific in 1977.

The crew are in a cabin only 2m wide.

In 1960, the submersible *Trieste* dived 10,916m – almost to the bottom of the Pacific's Mariana Trench. It took 4hrs, 48 minutes. The crew were housed in a steel sphere with walls 13cm thick. This stopped them being crushed by the huge pressure.

The crew of the Trieste were in the steel sphere below the sub.

Deep driller

A ship named the *JOIDES Resolution* has a huge drill that can bore into seabed 8,000m below. It removes cores (long cylinders) of rock. Studying the cores tells scientists how Earth's climate has changed during its history.

The drill ship JOIDES Resolution

Robosub

AUVs (Automated Underwater Vehicles) are robot submarines. *Autosub*, an AUV operated by scientists in Southampton, England, can work in areas that are otherwise hard to reach, such as under the polar ice.

Autosub (yellow) is launched from a crane.

*Deep-sea vents, see *Black smokers*, page 87

Ships and Shipwrecks

The first boats

The first boats were made by hollowing out tree trunks with fire or sharp tools. This is why they are called "dug-outs". The earliest known dug-out was found in Holland and is about 8,500 years old.

Sailing ships

The ancient Egyptians were the first people to use sails, 5,000 years ago. These first sails were square, and made of reeds.

The first sailing boats were used on the river Nile in Egypt.

! The first submarine was invented in 1620 by Cornelius van Drebbel, a Dutch doctor. Its wooden frame was covered in greased leather, and it was rowed by 12 oars. Tubes to the surface provided air. It could travel at depths of 5m for several hours.

The Vasa

In 1628, the Swedish warship *Vasa* first set sail. Unfortunately, its many guns made it top-heavy, and minutes later it toppled and sank. A third of its crew drowned. In 1956, the *Vasa*'s wreck was found. It was later raised and preserved.

It took a thousand oak trees to build the Vasa.

Finding the way

For many years, sailors navigated by the Sun, Moon and stars. They used instruments called sextants to plot the ship's position by measuring the height of the Sun or Moon above the horizon at certain times of day.

Sea speed

Speed at sea is measured in knots. One knot is one nautical mile (1.85km) per hour. To find a ship's speed, sailors in the past trailed a rope in the sea, knotted at even intervals. They counted the number of knots let out in 28 seconds.

A brass sextant

INTERNET LINKS
To find links to websites about ships, shipwrecks and more go to
www.usborne-quicklinks.com

Famous shipwreck	Date sank	Items recovered
Kyrenia ship (Greece)	4th century BC	400 wine jars; 10,000 almonds
La Trinidad Valencera (Spain)	1588	Bronze cannons each weighing 2.5 tonnes
Vergulde Draeck (Holland)	1656	8 chests full of silver
Whydah (America)	1717	Pirate treasure worth £250 million
Geldermalsen (Holland)	1752	Rare china crockery; gold ingots
HMS *Edinburgh* (Great Britain)	1942	5.5 tonnes of gold bars, worth £45 million

The *RMS Titanic* was 260m long and weighed over 53,000 tonnes. It was the largest ship of its day. The links of its anchor chains were 90cm long, and each weighed 80kg. Its main anchor was 4m long, and weighed 16 tonnes.

Iceberg ahoy!

Icebergs are a danger to ships because only about an eighth of the ice shows above the water. On the *Titanic*'s first voyage in 1912 she hit an iceberg in the north Atlantic and sank. Over 1,500 people died.

Titanic discovery

In 1977, Robert Ballard, an ocean scientist, tried to find the *Titanic*'s wreck. His attempt failed when all his equipment was lost at sea. Joining others, he returned in 1985. After five weeks' search, the *Titanic* was found 640km off north-east Canada.

The bow of the Titanic, viewed from a deep sea submersible

Fewer than a third of the Titanic's passengers escaped to safety.

Raft journey

Thor Heyerdahl's Kon-tiki at sea

In 1947, the explorer Thor Heyerdahl set out in his balsa-wood raft, the *Kon-tiki*, to sail from Peru to the Pacific Islands. He wanted to prove that Inca people could have made the trip 1,500 years ago, and populated the islands. His crew reached the island of Raroia in under four months.

Sea Travel Today

Sea traffic

Over 90% of goods transported around the world go by sea. So that sea traffic may travel smoothly, there are certain shipping routes, ("lanes"), in the oceans that ships usually follow.

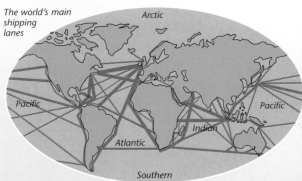

The world's main shipping lanes

Arctic

Pacific

Pacific

Indian

Atlantic

Southern

Parts of a ship

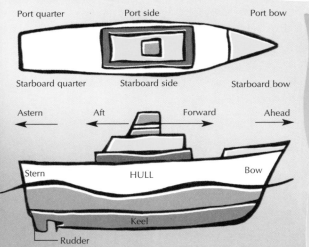

Port quarter   Port side   Port bow

Starboard quarter   Starboard side   Starboard bow

Astern   Aft   Forward   Ahead

Stern   HULL   Bow

Keel

Rudder

Sea cats

Catamarans are boats with two hulls. This means less of the boat touches water, reducing friction so it can travel more quickly. *The Cat* is a catamaran ferry with a real cutting edge. Its sharp bows pierce the waves, letting it speed to 70kph.

Enough shipping containers exist on the Earth to build a 5m high wall around the equator. Shipping containers are big metal boxes of a fixed size, mostly 6m or 12m long, used for carrying all kinds of cargo.

Shipping containers allow cargo to be loaded and unloaded quickly at ports.

The Cat runs between Maine, USA, and Nova Scotia, Canada.

BAY ferries

Buoys and marks

Ships stay safe by paying close attention to buoys, which are the roadsigns of the sea, and horn signals with special meanings:

Isolated danger mark

This buoy marks a dangerous area: avoid. Lights: two flashes

Safe water mark

This buoy marks a safe area. Lights: one long flash

Horn signals

One short blast:
Turning to starboard
Two short blasts:
Turning to port

Direction marks

Buoy	Direction of safe water	Lights (white)
	North	Continuous flashing
	East	Three quick flashes
	South	Six quick flashes + one long
	West	Nine quick flashes

INTERNET LINKS
To find links to websites about ships and shipping today, go to
www.usborne-quicklinks.com

Each year, lifeboats in the UK and Ireland alone save over 1,600 lives. All-weather class lifeboats are tough and totally watertight. If knocked over by fierce waves, they will bob upright almost immediately.

The UK and Ireland lifeboat services are run by volunteers.

Supertankers

The largest ships afloat are supertankers. They travel between the Middle East, Europe, America and Asia, each carrying enough oil to power a small city for a year. The *Jahre Viking* is the biggest: it is so long, its crew use bicycles to get around.

Stopping a supertanker is no easy task: it takes over 6km to bring the Jahre Viking to a halt.

Vessel record	Name	Statistics
Largest vessel	*ULCC* Jahre Viking* (oil supertanker)	458m long; can carry 4.1 million oil barrels
Largest warship	*USS Harry S. Truman* (aircraft carrier)	334m long; flight deck 18,211m²
Largest cruise liner	*Voyager of the Seas*	310m long; can carry 3,114 passengers
Water speed	*Spirit of Australia* (hydroplane)	Reached a speed of 511kph (1978)
Largest sailing ship	*Royal Clipper*	42 sails, using 5,202m² of canvas

*ULCC: *Ultra Large Crude Carrier*

Ocean Resources

Sea harvest

Each year, some 90 million tonnes of fish are caught in the oceans. Over half comes from the Pacific. In 1986, a Norwegian boat took over 120 million fish in a single catch: enough for each Norwegian to have 26 each.

Most caught fish	Caught in 2000
Peruvian anchovy	11.3 million tonnes
Alaska pollock	3.0 million tonnes
Atlantic herring	2.3 million tonnes
Skipjack tuna	1.9 million tonnes
Japanese anchovy	1.7 million tonnes
Chilean jack mackerel	1.5 million tonnes

Atlantic

Pacific

Indian

Pacific

Southern

The pink areas on this map show the parts of the ocean where most of the world's fish are caught.

INTERNET LINKS
To find links to websites about the resources of the seas and oceans, go to **www.usborne-quicklinks.com**

Seaweed sandwich

Seaweed is full of vitamins and calcium. In China and Japan huge amounts are harvested and eaten. In Ireland it is spread over the fields as fertilizer. Seaweed is also used to thicken ice cream and to make shampoo, toothpaste and even explosives.

Seaweed... yum!

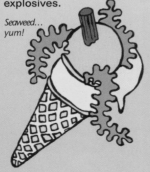

Gold mine

Sea water contains about 400 times more gold than is owned on land. Sea gold has already been mined on the coasts of Alaska. If all the sea gold was mined, there would be enough for everyone on Earth to have a piece weighing over 4kg.

Fish farming

Many countries breed fish in undersea farms. On fish farms, plaice grow to full size in 18-24 months: half the time it takes in the wild. They are also easier to catch than in the open sea.

A Norwegian salmon farm

About 66 million tonnes of salt are taken from the sea each year. In hot countries, it is done by drying sea water in huge pans left in the Sun.

The sea salt produced in a year would make a pile nearly three times as high as Egypt's Great Pyramid.

Ocean oil

Over a fifth of the world's oil comes from the seabed. Oil formed millions of years ago from the bodies of tiny sea animals and plants which drifted to the sea bed and were covered in layers of mud and sand.

Offshore oil producers	Barrels produced daily
Norway	3,230,000
Mexico	2,500,000
UK	2,180,000
Saudi Arabia	1,990,000
United Arab Emirates	1,150,000
USA	1,060,000

Taming the tides

Scientists are now looking to the sea as a source of energy. The world's first tidal power station was built on the River Rance in France. A dam with 24 tunnels in it runs across the river mouth. As the tides rush in and out, they turn generators in the tunnels which produce electricity.

Each of the 24 generators at the Rance tidal power station makes enough power to light a medium-sized town.

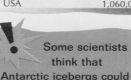

Some scientists think that Antarctic icebergs could provide desert areas with fresh water. Boats could tow large icebergs to Africa, for example. Wrapping the icebergs in plastic could contain the ice that melts.

Icebergs – the answer to drought in hot countries?

Deep sea nodules

A quarter of the Pacific Ocean floor is covered in black, potato-sized lumps, or nodules. These contain valuable metals, such as nickel and manganese. Over millions of years the nodules grow in layers around small objects, such as grains of sand or even sharks' teeth.

Black lumps like these litter the ocean floor.

Priceless poo

Sea bird droppings, or guano, are the world's most valuable natural fertilizer – 30 times richer than farmyard manure. For thousands of years, millions of cormorants have nested on Peru's cliffs. At times, parts of the cliffs were covered in a layer of guano 50m thick.

Cormorant droppings are used as fertilizer.

Oceans in Danger

Over 80% of the waste polluting the oceans comes from the land. Here are some of the main causes of pollution:

- Sewage pumped into the sea
- Nuclear waste from power plants
- Poisonous metals, such as mercury, tin and lead, from factories, mines and boats
- Chemical fertilizers and pesticides, washed off farmland and carried by rivers to the sea.
- Oil and petrol are washed off the land into the sea. Oil also comes from oil rig and tanker accidents.

Oil ruins seabirds' feathers, and they die of cold.

A striped dolphin caught in a drift net

Sick slick

In March 1989, the oil tanker, *Exxon Valdez*, ran aground in Prince William Sound, Alaska. In one of the worst oil spills ever, 45 million litres of oil poured into the sea, killing hundreds of thousands of sea birds and animals.

The Exxon Valdez oilspill

Plastic drift nets are trailed across the ocean like giant walls: just one net may be 20km long. Each year, thousands of sea mammals and birds die when they become entangled in drift nets used for catching squid.

Fight to survive

The Mediterranean monk seal is Europe's most endangered mammal. The have been killed for their meat and skins, and by fishermen who see them as pests.

Plenty more fish in the sea?

Fish are being taken from the world's oceans faster than they can breed. This is called overfishing. Off Canada's east coast, for example, fishing Atlantic cod is banned, as very few remain.

In some countries, nets with a large mesh are used to let young fish escape.

Fewer th 400 Mediterran monk seals rem

INTERNET LINKS
To find links to websites about the dangers threatening the oceans, go to **www.usborne-quicklinks.com**

Suffocated sea

In summer, seas polluted with waste fertilizer and sewage may be covered in a thick, green slime of phytoplankton*. The plankton uses minerals in the waste to grow. It blocks out sunlight other sea plants need. As it rots, it uses up so much oxygen that many sea creatures suffocate.

Phytoplankton comes in many shapes and sizes.

The name "penguin" was first given to a now-extinct North Atlantic bird, later called the great auk. What we call penguins were named after these birds because they looked like them.

The great auk could not fly, so it was easy to hunt. The last one was killed in 1844.

*See page 82

Endangered sea animals	Population	Major threats
Blue whale	Under 4,000	Pollution; some hunting
Fin whale	50–100,000	Pollution
Kemp's Ridley turtle	Under 4,000	Shrimp fishing nets
Florida manatee	Under 3,500	Killed by motor boats
Juan Fernandez fur seal	About 12,000	Hunting
Sea otter	Under 2,500	Hunting; oil pollution

Marine park

The Great Barrier Reef is home to 400 species of coral and 1,500 species of fish. In 1980, the Barrier Reef Marine Park was set up to protect the reef from tourists, pollution and overfishing. There are now special areas set aside for nesting sites, research, fishing and tourists.

Scientists believe that, unless action is taken to save them, more than half of the world's coral reefs could be destroyed by 2030.

Law of the sea

The Law of the Sea aims to protect the sea and control how it is used. It was drawn up by the United Nations in 1982. It divides the sea up into areas for different countries, leaving about two thirds of the open ocean free for all.

The Future of the Sea

Able cable

The Internet's future lies in the world's longest undersea fibre-optic telecoms cable. Called *Sea-Me-We 3*, it runs for 39,000km, and connects countries from Germany to Japan and Australia. It can carry the equivalent of 4,000 encyclopedias' worth of information in a second.

Water power

Ocean Thermal Energy Conversion (OTEC) makes energy from tropical seas. Warm surface water is pumped into a special ship, where it warms tanks of an easy-boiling liquid. The gas produced drives turbines, making electricity. Cold water is then pumped in to cool the gas back to liquid, and the process restarts.

Cold water pumped in here

OTEC ships could make energy if oil and gas reserves ever run low.

Deep Flight

Submersibles must lose or gain weight to rise and sink. This limits their speed. Graham Hawkes*, a leading inventor of manned submersibles, is building speedy "Deep Flight" subs that stay the same weight, but fly like planes.

If built, the futuristic Deep Flight II will take explorers to the deepest parts of the ocean.

Deep Flight subs have stubby, upside-down wings for speeding down into the depths of the sea.

A ship up-ended is usually bad news, but scientists in the USA have a ship that flips on purpose. *R/V FLIP* flips and floats upright, cutting out wave noise so its crew can study undersea sounds. When it flips, the crew walk on its walls! Longer "flip ships" may one day be built to work in deeper seas.

Don't worry – it's meant to do this

Farming the seas

Overfishing (see page 116) is seriously reducing the world's fish population. Fish farming, already common in places such as Norway, could help numbers grow again. In the future, more fish may be farmed than are caught in the wild.

 Turn to page 108 to see Graham Hawkes in the Wasp, a diving suit he designed.

INTERNET LINKS
To find links to websites about the future
of the oceans, and living under the sea,
go to **www.usborne-quicklinks.com**

Living underwater

Aquarius is an undersea
laboratory off the coast
of Florida, USA. It lets
scientists live and work
in the ocean without
having to keep returning
to a ship on the surface.
We may not see huge
undersea cities in the
future, but there may
well be more labs – and
even holiday resorts!

Robolobster!

In the future, robots modelled on sea
creatures may save lives. A robot
lobster, built in the USA, may be the
first of an army of robots which scuttle
over the seafloor, sniffing out deadly
mines with electronic feelers.

*This robot
lobster can
walk in any
direction, just
like a real
lobster.*

Medicines that may
help to fight cancer
have been made from
substances found in
coral, sponges and
other sealife. If we are
careful to protect the
world's sealife, we may
yet discover new cures
to many diseases.

*Inside Aquarius, the world's only
undersea research laboratory.*

*Corals have proved to contain
cancer-fighting chemicals.*

Floating city

Plans to build the largest cruise liner ever are
now underway. Called the *Freedom Ship*, it
will be 1.3km long, 25 storeys high, and house
50,000 people. It will be more like a city than
a cruise liner, with shops, schools, parks,
cafés, and its own airstrip. Unlike
any city, though, it will circle
the world once every
two years.

*If built, the Freedom
Ship will be the
biggest ship
ever.*

Sea Myths and Legends

The kraken

Norse legends tell of a huge sea monster, the kraken, which could turn a ship over. It was a cross between an octopus and a squid, with suckers, claws, and a beak strong enough to bore through wood.

The kraken legend may well be based on a giant squid.

Lost continent

The continent of Atlantis is said to have flourished in about 10,000 BC. It was then destroyed in a volcanic eruption, and sank without trace. No one knows if Atlantis really existed, but there are many theories about its location. These include the Greek island of Santorini, an island near Gibraltar, Cuba and Antarctica.

Ghost ship

The *Flying Dutchman* is said to bring bad luck to all who see her. The ship left Amsterdam for the East Indies in the 17th century. On the way back, she met a fierce storm. Her arrogant captain swore to the devil that he would sail through the storm, even if he had to sail until Judgement Day. His ship never returned. It is said that the ship was doomed to haunt the seas forever.

The Flying Dutchman was sighted during World War II by German submariners.

"Crossing the line" is an old custom on ships passing the equator. Those on board who have not crossed before ("pollywogs") are called before King Neptune and his court, played by the crew, who punish them for their "crimes", often by shaving and soaking them. They are then called "shellbacks".

King Neptune's sceptre is a three-pronged spear called a trident.

Abandoned ship

In 1872, a ship called the *Mary Celeste* was found drifting in the Atlantic. The whole crew had vanished, apparently in a hurry, leaving their boots. The lifeboats were also missing, but, to this day, no one knows for sure what happened to them.

INTERNET LINKS
To find links to websites about ocean myths and legends go to **www.usborne-quicklinks.com**

Dolphin rescue

A Greek legend tells how dolphins saved the life of the musician, Arion. He was sailing back to Greece after winning a music competition in Italy. The ship's crew wanted his prizes, and attacked him. They allowed him to play one last tune, which attracted a school of dolphins. Arion leapt overboard and was safely carried home on the dolphins' backs.

Ocean gods	Worshippers
Poseidon	Greeks
Neptune	Romans
Njörd	Norse
T'ien Hou (goddess of sailors)	Chinese
O-Wata-Tsu-Mi	Japanese
Tangaroa	Polynesians
Sedna	Inuit
Manannán mac Lir	Celts

Pictures of dolphins, like these, were often painted on ancient Greek pottery.

In ancient Greece, dolphins were sacred to the god Apollo, and it was illegal to harm them.

Clam creation

In Polynesian myth, the world was created in a giant clam. A goddess, Old Spider, squeezed inside a giant clam and found two snails and a worm. She made the smaller snail the Moon, and the larger one the Sun. Half the clam shell became the Earth, the other half the sky, and the worm's salty sweat became the sea.

Very like a whale?

In 1852, two whaling ships, the *Monongahela* and the *Rebecca Sims*, harpooned what they thought was a whale, 4,000km west of Ecuador. When they hauled it in, they were amazed. It seemed to be a brownish-grey reptile, 45m long, with huge jaws full of sharp, curving teeth. The body was too huge to keep, so they cut off its head and preserved it in salt. The ships then headed home, but only the *Rebecca Sims* made it: the *Monongahela*, and the monster's head, were never seen again.

Do sea serpents really exist?

121

Ocean Records

The oceans that cover two-thirds of our planet are full of record-breaking features and creatures. This map shows some of them.

Arctic Ocean
Smallest ocean:
14,090,000km²

Longest undersea telecoms cable
Sea-Me-We 3 cable network:
39,000km

Hottest surface sea water
Persian Gulf:
35.6°C in summer

Saltiest sea water
Red Sea
(4.2% salt)

Deepest point on Earth
Challenger Deep, Mariana Trench: 11,022m

Indian Ocean

Smallest sea fish
Dwarf goby: max. length 8.9mm

Atlantic Ocean

Largest seabird
Wandering albatross:
3.5m wingspan

Longest coral reef:
Great Barrier Reef:
2,028km

Key to seas

1. South China Sea
2. Mediterranean Sea
3. Arabian Sea
4. Weddell Sea
5. Bering Sea
6. Caribbean Sea
7. Gulf of Mexico
8. Sea of Okhotsk
9. Sea of Japan
10. North Sea
11. Black Sea
12. Sargasso Sea

122

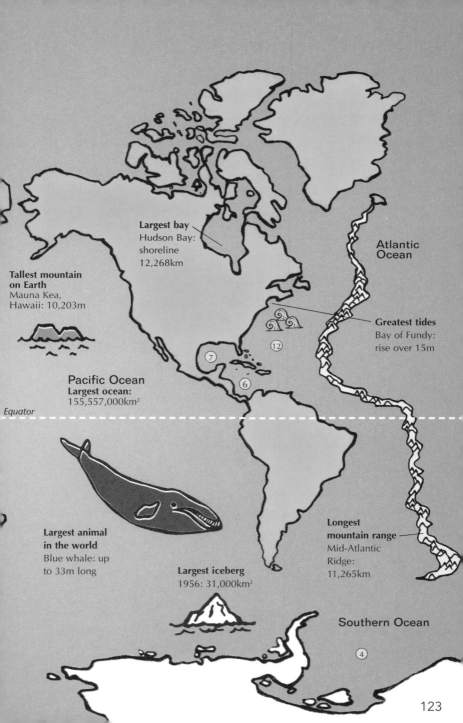

Largest bay
Hudson Bay:
shoreline
12,268km

Atlantic
Ocean

**Tallest mountain
on Earth**
Mauna Kea,
Hawaii: 10,203m

Greatest tides
Bay of Fundy:
rise over 15m

⑫

⑦

⑥

Pacific Ocean
Largest ocean:
155,557,000km²

Equator

**Largest animal
in the world**
Blue whale: up
to 33m long

**Longest
mountain range**
Mid-Atlantic
Ridge:
11,265km

Largest iceberg
1956: 31,000km²

Southern Ocean

④

Seas and Oceans Quiz

So, is your head swimming with ocean facts? Do you know your krill from your kraken? Take our quiz to find out how much of a salty sea dog you really are...

Answers on page 128

1 The sea is blue because:

A it reflects blue light rays

B it is coloured by mud

C it is cold

D water is blue

(See page 70)

2 Sound moving through sea water travels:

A twice as slowly

B twice as quickly

C four times as slowly

D four times as quickly

(See page 71)

3 170 million years ago there was one vast ocean on Earth, known as:

A Pacific

B Pangaea

C Panthalassa

D Pantomime

(See page 72)

4 Earth's deepest point is:

A the Mid-Atlantic Ridge

B the Mariana Trench

C the Tonga Trench

D the abyssal plain

(See page 75)

5 Spring tides happen:

A in the spring

B twice a day

C twice a month

D when the Sun and Moon are at right angles

(See page 76)

6 Tsunamis are caused by:

A the Moon's gravity

B the Sun's gravity

C undersea earthquakes or eruptions

D Godzilla

(See page 77)

7 The longest coastline is:

A Russia's

B Canada's

C Greenland's

D Indonesia's

(See page 78)

8 The Great Barrier Reef:

A is 10,000km long

B is visible from the Moon

C is being eaten by giant clams

D is off the Austrian coast

(See page 81)

9 Krill are:

A a type of whale

B phytoplankton

C tiny, shrimp-like animals

D very poisonous

(See page 83)

10 Which of these deep-sea fish doesn't have lights on its body?

A angler fish

B lantern fish

C flashlight fish

D hagfish

(See page 85)

11 The most common animal in deep-sea trenches is the:

A gulper eel

B sea cucumber

C sea spider

D rat-tail

(See page 86)

12 Torpedo rays defend themselves by:

A wrapping themselves in a slimy cocoon

B rolling into a ball

C giving electric shocks

D leaving their arms behind

(See page 88)

13 The fastest fish is the:

A marlin

B sailfish

C barracuda

D swordfish

(See page 89)

14 The blue whale is:

A the world's biggest fish

B the earliest known whale

C the biggest pinniped

D the biggest animal ever

(See page 90)

15 Manatees belong to the mammal group called the:

A pinnipeds

B cetaceans

C carnivores

D sirenians

(See page 90)

16 The largest crustacean is:
A the American lobster
B the Japanese spider crab
C the giant squid
D the giant clam
(*See page 92*)

17 The world's fastest sea bird is:
A the frigate bird
B the gentoo penguin
C the wandering albatross
D the Arctic tern
(*See page 94*)

18 Atlantic green turtles lay their eggs:
A in the Sargasso Sea
B on Ascension Island
C on Bouvet Island
D in the Amazon River
(*See page 99*)

19 The warmest ocean is:
A the Atlantic
B the Pacific
C the Indian
D the Southern
(*See page 100*)

20 The Arctic Ocean:
A is usually frozen
B freezes at 0°C
C flows clockwise around Antarctica
D is the deepest ocean
(*See page 102*)

21 The bay with the longest shoreline is:
A Hudson Bay
B the Bay of Bengal
C the Bay of Biscay
D the Bay of Fundy
(*See page 123*)

22 The largest ocean is:
A the Atlantic
B the Pacific
C the Indian
D the Southern
(*See page 96*)

23 Penguins:
A live north of the equator
B are found in Antarctica
C fly south in the winter
D extend their flippers to stay warm
(*See page 104*)

24 The first Viking in America was probably:
A Eric the Red
B Leaf the Green
C Leif the Lucky
D Roald the Bold
(*See page 106*)

25 Christopher Columbus sailed from Spain seeking:
A a route to Asia
B America
C the Bahamas
D mermaids
(*See page 106*)

26 Which vessel dived into the Mariana Trench in 1960?
A *Nautilus*
B *Triton*
C *Trieste*
D *Kaiko*
(*See page 109*)

27 The *Titanic*'s wreck was discovered in:
A 1947
B 1956
C 1977
D 1985
(*See page 111*)

28 The starboard quarter of a ship is at the:
A front left
B front right
C back left
D back right
(*See page 112*)

29 When a ship gives two short blasts on its horn:
A it's turning to port
B it's turning to starboard
C it's going straight ahead
D it's warning of danger
(*See page 113*)

30 The most-caught fish in the year 2000 was the:
A Atlantic herring
B Patagonian toothfish
C Peruvian anchovy
D Japanese anchovy
(*See page 114*)

31 Europe's most endangered mammal is the:
A great auk
B Mediterranean monk seal
C sea otter
D blue whale
(*See page 117*)

32 The legendary ghost ship said to bring bad luck is the:
A *Mary Celeste*
B *Monongahela*
C *Flying Dutchman*
D *Golden Hind*
(*See page 120*)

33 Dolphins were sacred to which Greek god?
A Zeus
B Apollo
C Hermes
D Pan
(*See page 121*)

Glossary

abyssal plain A vast, flat area of the ocean floor, below 4,000m.

abyssal zone The ocean depths lying between 4,000m and 6,000m below sea level.

ACV Air Cushion Vehicle, for example, a hovercraft.

ADS Atmospheric Diving Suit: a hard, deep-diving suit with built-in air supply.

algae A group of simple water plants, ranging from tiny, one-celled plankton to giant seaweed.

atoll A circular or horseshoe-shaped coral island with a shallow lagoon at its centre.

AUV Autonomous Underwater Vehicle: a robot submersible.

bacteria A group of very tiny, one-celled living things, invisible to the naked eye, some of which may cause disease.

barnacle A small crustacean that sticks tightly to undersea objects and animals.

bathysphere A metal sphere used in early deep-sea exploration.

black smoker A chimney, formed from minerals, around a deep-sea vent.

blue-green bacteria An ancient group of water-dwelling bacteria which, like plants, can make food from sunlight.

bow The front part of a ship or boat.

cetaceans A group of sea mammals with no rear limbs, including whales and dolphins.

continental shelf The shallow seabed around the continents, usually no deeper than 200m below sea level.

continental slope The sloping area leading from the continental shelf to the abyssal plain.

crustaceans A group of animals with hard shells and jointed legs, such as lobsters and shrimp.

current A huge band of water running through the sea.

dinoflagellates Tiny, one-celled sea plants. Some are poisonous; others produce their own light.

DSV Deep Submergence Vehicle: a deep-sea submersible.

equator An imaginary circle dividing the northern and southern halves of the Earth.

erosion The process by which rock or soil is worn away by wind or water.

extinct Living things that haven't been seen for 50 years, and so are believed to have died out, are said to be extinct.

hadal zone The deepest ocean depths, reaching from 6,000m below sea level down into the deepest trenches.

hull The main body of a ship or boat.

hydroplane A motorboat with an underside shaped to lift its bow out of the water at high speeds.

invertebrate An animal without a backbone.

knot A measurement of speed at sea. One knot is equal to 1.85kph.

lagoon A shallow lake cut off from the sea by a barrier such as a coral reef or sand bank.

lava Molten rock above the seabed or land.

magma Molten rock underneath the seabed or land.

mammal A warm-blooded vertebrate with hair that feeds its young on milk.

midnight zone (or bathyal zone) The ocean depths lying between 1,000m and 4,000m below sea level.

migration A stage in some animals' lives when they travel a long way to find food or to breed.

molluscs A large group of invertebrates, often with shells, ranging from limpets to giant squid.

neap tide A very low tide that occurs twice monthly, at the Moon's first and last quarters, when the Moon is at right angles to the Sun.

oceanography The scientific study of the oceans and seas.

overfishing Removing fish from the seas more quickly than they can breed and replace their numbers.

Pangaea A single, giant landmass that began to break up about 225 millon years ago, leading to the continents we know today.

Panthalassa The vast ocean that surrounded the single super-continent of Pangaea.

parasite A living thing that lives and feeds upon another, often causing it harm, for example, a flea.

phytoplankton Tiny, drifting sea plants.

pinnipeds A group of sea mammals including seals, sealions and walruses.

plankton Tiny sea plants and animals that drift near the sea's surface.

plate A piece of the Earth's hard outer shell.

polyp A small sea invertebrate. Coral is made from millions of hard polyp skeletons.

predator An animal that hunts, kills and eats other animals.

ROV Remotely Operated Vehicle: an undersea vehicle operated from, and fastened to, a ship.

seamount A volcano under the sea.

seaquake An earthquake under the sea.

sediment Mud, sand and rock that settles on the seabed.

siphonophore A jellyfish-like animal, such as a Portuguese man-of-war, that is made up of a colony of tiny animals.

sonar (**so**und, **na**vigation and **ra**nging) A device used by ships to find the position of underwater objects by sending sounds and measuring echoes.

spreading ridge An undersea mountain range, formed when lava rises to fill cracks in the sea floor.

spring tide A very high tide that occurs twice monthly, at the Full and New Moon, when the Moon is lined up with the Sun.

stern The back part of a ship or boat.

subduction zone An area where two tectonic plates crash into each other, and one plate is pushed underneath the other.

submersible A small, freely moving submarine used by ocean scientists.

sunlit zone The top 200m of the ocean, where there is enough sunlight for sea plants to live.

tectonic plate *See* **plate**

Tethys Sea A large sea that jutted into the super-continent of Pangaea.

trench A deep, V-shaped dip in the seabed, formed at a subduction zone.

tsunami A large wave caused by a seaquake or an undersea eruption.

turbidity current An avalanche of mud and sand, which may be caused by a seaquake.

twilight zone The ocean depths lying between 200m and 1,000m below sea level.

vent An opening in the seabed through which mineral-rich water, heated inside the Earth, gushes into the ocean.

vertebrate An animal with a backbone.

zooplankton Tiny, drifting sea animals.

Acknowledgements

Every effort has been made to trace the copyright holders of the material in this book. If any rights have been omitted, the publishers offer to rectify this in any subsequent editions following notification. The publishers are grateful to the following organizations and individuals for their permission to reproduce material (t=top, m=middle, b=bottom, l=left, r=right):

AP Photo/Michel Lipchitz: **111mr**
Bay Ferries: **112b**
Corbis: **74ml** Ralph A. Clevenger/CORBIS; **79l** Wolfgang Kaeler/CORBIS; **83tr** Douglas P. Wilson, Frank Lane Picture Agency/CORBIS; **87tl** Ralph White/CORBIS; **89m** Jeffrey L. Rottman/CORBIS; **92ml** Richard Cummins/CORBIS; **93b** Stephen Frink/CORBIS; **96-97 main** Nik Wheeler/CORBIS; **100m** Tony Arruza/CORBIS; **101b** Charles O'Rear/CORBIS; **102br** Dan Guravich/CORBIS; **103ml** Winifred Wisniewski, Frank Lane Picture Agency/CORBIS; **107mr** Ralph White/CORBIS; **111m** Ralph White/CORBIS; **112mr** Wolfgang Kaehler/CORBIS; **114mr** Paul A. Souders/CORBIS; **115ml** Yann Arthus-Bertrand/CORBIS; **br** Academy of Natural Sciences of Philadelphia/CORBIS; **117bl** Academy of Natural Sciences of Philadelphia/CORBIS
Courtesy of the Naval Historical Centre: **109mr**
Dr David Billett, Southampton Oceanography Centre: **86bl**
Digital Vision: **Title page; Half-title; 70mr; 71; 72-73; 77; 78m; 80-81b; 91mr; 92bl; 94m; 97tr; 98bl; br; bl; 104br; 104-105 main; 115tr; 116tr; 117br**
Dirk H.R. Spennemann, Albury NSW, Australia: **96br**
Freedom Ship International Inc.: **119b**
Getty Images: **92t** Stuart Westmorland
Prof. Gwyn Griffiths, Southampton Oceanography Centre: **109br**
Hawkes Ocean Technologies: **118m**
INCAT, Australia: **112b**
Jahre Dahl Bergesen: **113m**
Jan Witting, Northeastern University, Massachussets: **119tr**
Jeffrey Jeffords (**Divegallery.com**): **81r; 82b; 83r; 96m; 99br**
National Oceanic and Atmospheric Administration (NOAA)/Dept of Commerce: **76bl; 80ml; 83ml; 87r; bl; 89tl; 92mr; 99tr; ml; 100bl; 103mr; 105m; 107t; m; 108br; 115mr; 119ml**
NOAA/National Geophysical Data Centre: **108bl**
National Ocean Service (NOS) Photo Gallery: **78bl** Laura Francis/NOS; **88bl** Daniel Gotshall/NOS; **116m** Ocean Drilling Program/Texas A&M University: **108bl**
Prof. Paul Tyler, Southampton Oceanography Centre/Prof. Craig Young, Harbor Branch Oceanographic Institute, Fort Pierce, Florida: **85b; mr**
RNLI/Robert Townsend: **113tr**
Science Photo Library: **75br** Astrid & Hanns-Frieder Michler/Science Photo Library
Scripps Institution of Oceanography: **118bm**
Sea Solar Power International: illustration on **118tr** based on their SSP 100 MW plantship
Stockbyte: **80-81b; 119mr**
Vasa Museum, Stockholm, Sweden: **110m**

Additional illustrators Mike Barber, Trevor Boyer, Peter Dennis, John Francis, Nigel Frey, Jeremy Gower, Laura Hammonds, David Hancock, Alan Harris, Phillip Hood, Christine Howes, Ian Jackson, Chris Lyon, Malcolm McGregor, David Quinn, Michael Roffe, Luke Sargent, Chris Shields, Karen Tomlins

Quiz Answers
1A, 2D, 3C, 4B, 5C, 6C, 7B, 8B, 9C, 10D, 11B, 12C, 13B, 14D, 15D, 16B, 17A, 18B, 19C, 20A, 21A, 22B, 23B, 24C, 25A, 26C, 27D, 28D, 29A, 30C, 31B, 32C, 33B

DINOSAURS
AND
PREHISTORY

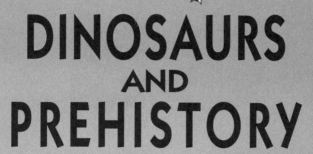

DINOSAURS
AND
PREHISTORY

Sarah Khan

Edited by Phillip Clarke

Designed by
Luke Sargent and Karen Tomlins

Digital imagery by Keith Furnival

Consultants: Dr David Martill,
University of Portsmouth
and Darren Naish

Internet Links

Throughout this book, we have suggested interesting websites where you can find out more about the prehistoric world. To visit the sites, go to the **Usborne Quicklinks website** at **www.usborne-quicklinks.com** and type the keywords "book of facts". There you will find links to click on to take you to all the sites. Here are some of the things you can do on the websites:

 Swim with prehistoric sharks.

 Play a game to find out how you would survive as a dinosaur.

 Travel back in time to the last Ice Age.

 Uncover the mysteries of an ancient Turkish village.

Computer not essential

If you don't have access to the Internet, don't worry. This book is complete on its own.

Prehistory Contents

What is Prehistory?

History is the story of human beings that is learned from written records. It goes back about 5,500 years to the first known writing.

Prehistory is even older than that. It is the story of life on Earth that is learned from the remains of animals and plants. Prehistory begins around 3,000 million years ago with the first known living things.

The Sun's heat and light made life on Earth possible.

Fit for life

It took millions of years for conditions on Earth to become suitable for life to begin. To survive, living things need the right amounts of light and heat from the Sun, along with food, water and oxygen.

4,600 million years ago

A cloud of dust and gases swirling round the Sun started to shrink and heat up. It then changed into a ball of liquid rock.

4,000 million years ago

The ball of rock slowly cooled down to form the Earth. Thick clouds gathered over the surface and rain began to fall.

3,500 million years ago

It rained for thousands of years. The rainwater made rivers and oceans.

3,000 million years ago

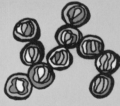

The first living things grew in the sea. They were made of just one cell each and were similar to bacteria or germs.

INTERNET LINK

For a link to a website where you can take an interactive tour through the story of the universe go to **www.usborne-quicklinks.com**

The Earth was formed 4,600 million years ago. If you counted to 4,600 million and each number took you one second to recite, you would be counting for over 146 years.

Measuring time

The Earth's story goes back so far that scientists measure it in periods of millions of years. Dates in prehistory cannot be exact, but they give the order in which events are thought to have happened.

In 1650, Archbishop James Ussher calculated from the Bible that the Earth was created on Sunday, October 23rd, 4004BC. Today, some people still believe in his date, though most scientists do not.

James Ussher believed he knew when the Earth was created.

Earth's time chart - in seconds

This time chart shows Earth's story since it was formed 4,600 million years ago. It counts each year as if it were only one second.

Formation of the Earth	146 years ago	
Earliest known living cells	100 years ago	
Jellyfish, corals, sponges	18 years ago	
Early reptiles	10 years ago	
Dinosaurs, early mammals	6 years ago	
First apes	1 year ago	
Modern human beings	11 hours ago	
Beginning of civilization	2¾ hours ago	
Egyptian pyramids built	1¼ hours ago	
Birth of Jesus Christ	33 minutes ago	
Columbus landed in America	8½ minutes ago	
Men landed on the Moon	33 seconds ago	

How Do We Know?

Any information we have about prehistory comes from fossils. Fossils are the remains of animals and plants that have become embedded in a hard substance such as rock. Every fossil is a clue to what life was like millions of years ago.

This ammonite fossil is over 65 million years old

A small chance

The chance of a fossil being found is very small:

• The rock in which it lies must be raised to the surface.

• Wind and rain must then wear the rock away to expose the fossil.

• The fossil must be discovered soon after that before it is worn away.

A fossil is as old as the rock in which it is found. This means that any fossils found in the very bottom layer of rock in the Grand Canyon, USA, will be 2,000 million years old.

Types of fossil

There are three types of fossil:

Body fossils are the actual parts of a prehistoric plant or animal, including any casts or moulds that are made of the dead body. Most body fossils found are of the hard parts of animals such as:

Teeth

Shells

Bones

Fossils of soft body parts are rarely found because these tissues decay easily.

Trace fossils are the imprints or marks made by prehistoric plants and animals while they were still alive, rather than after death. They include:

Skin

Footprints

Droppings

Molecular fossils are chemical traces of prehistoric plants and animals. Scientists crush the rocks which contain the traces so that they can dissolve out and analyse the chemicals.

Becoming a fossil

There are many ways in which a plant or animal can turn into a fossil:

• A small animal or plant becomes trapped in a substance that turns hard.

This prehistoric insect is trapped in amber.

• Minerals seep into rocks, replacing the soft tissues of a buried plant or animal. The mineral forms a rock-like fossil.

• The hard parts of a plant or animal dissolve, leaving only a substance called carbon.

• The hard parts of a plant or animal are replaced by minerals.

• A buried plant or animal dissolves, leaving an impression which may be filled in to make a cast.

This is a fossilized impression of a prehistoric birch leaf.

Living fossils

Many types of animal and plant, such as ferns, dragonflies and some sharks, have changed very little for millions of years. They are called living fossils.*

Great White Shark

Megalodon

Today's Great White Sharks look like much smaller versions of their prehistoric ancestors, called Megalodons.

La Brea Tar Pits, USA, is home to over three million fossils, the oldest of which date back 40,000 years. Tar pits form when oil seeps to the Earth's surface and evaporates, leaving sticky pools. Animals such as lions, wolves and mammoths became trapped in the La Brea pit and their remains were preserved.

Mammoth in a sticky situation

INTERNET LINK

For a link to a website where you can watch prehistoric animals turn into fossils in a variety of ways go to **www.usborne-quicklinks.com**

Dating fossils

Scientists can work out the age of any fossil up to 100,000 years old by using a process called carbon dating. All living things absorb and then give out rays of carbon particles. After death, the rays are given out at a steady rate. By counting the rays, it is possible to tell how old the fossil is.

Living person	2,500 particle rays per hour
5,600 year old fossil	1,250 particle rays per hour
11,200 year old fossil	625 particle rays per hour
44,000 year old fossil	3 particle rays per hour

* See page 186

Time Trail

Each period of Earth's story has a name. This chart shows the major events that occurred during each period. In this chart (and throughout this book), mya stands for "million years ago".

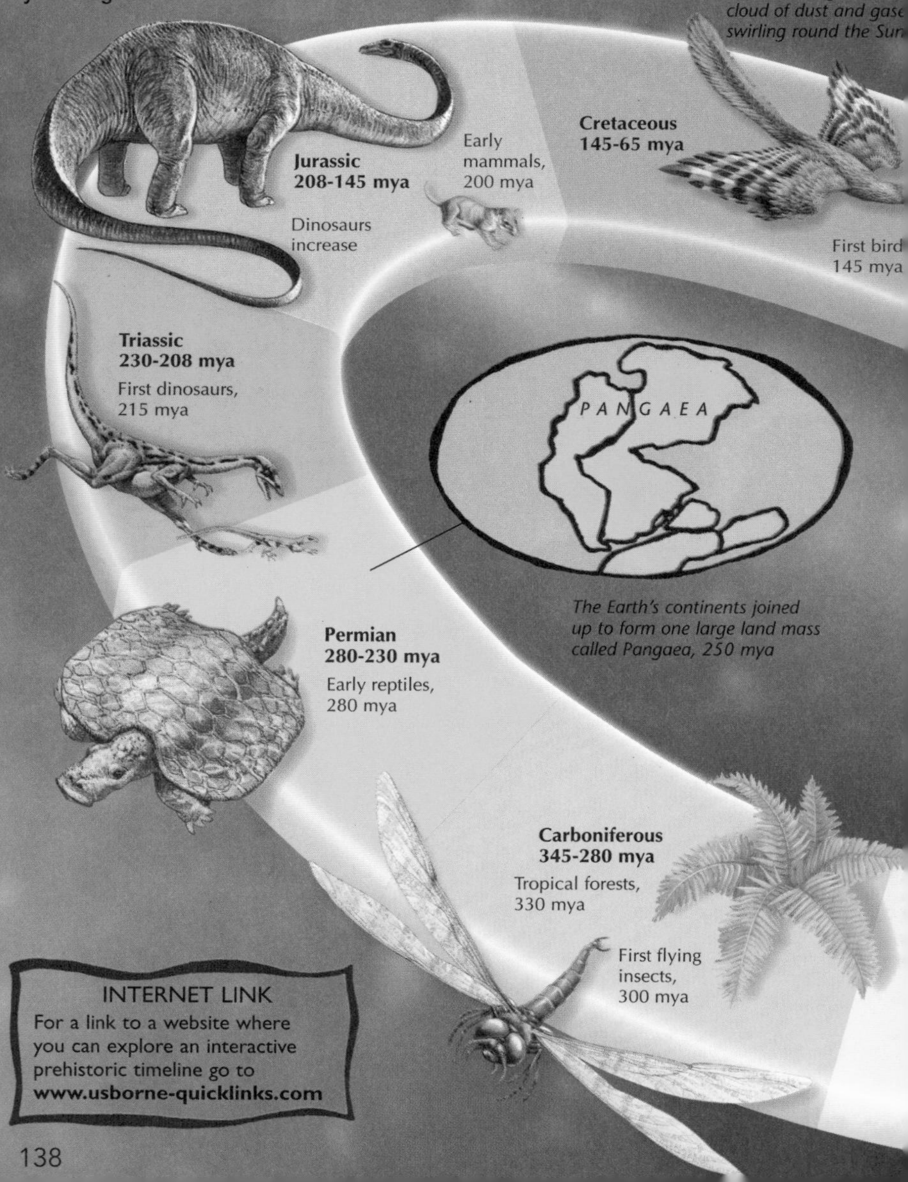

The Earth began as a cloud of dust and gases swirling round the Sun

**Cretaceous
145-65 mya**

**Jurassic
208-145 mya**

Dinosaurs increase

Early mammals, 200 mya

First bird
145 mya

**Triassic
230-208 mya**

First dinosaurs, 215 mya

PANGAEA

The Earth's continents joined up to form one large land mass called Pangaea, 250 mya

**Permian
280-230 mya**

Early reptiles, 280 mya

**Carboniferous
345-280 mya**

Tropical forests, 330 mya

First flying insects, 300 mya

INTERNET LINK
For a link to a website where you can explore an interactive prehistoric timeline go to
www.usborne-quicklinks.com

Fossils from 208-145 mya were first found in the European Jura mountains, which is why that period is now known as the Jurassic. Many periods on this timescale are named after the places where fossils from that time were first discovered.

-ambrian -570 mya

Formation of the Earth, 4,600 mya

First known living things, 3,200 mya

First ice age, 2,300 mya

First animals, 680 mya

First shellfish, 570 mya

Cambrian 570-500 mya

Palaeocene 65-55 mya

Earliest primates, 60 mya

Eocene 55-38 mya
Mammals increase.

Oligocene 38-22 mya
Earliest apes, 30 mya

Miocene 22-6 mya
Grazing animals increase.

First arthropods, 570 mya

First fish, 540 mya

Ordovician 500-435 mya
First plants live on land, 420 mya

Pliocene, 6-2 mya
First human beings, 2 mya

Pleistocene, 2 mya-10,000 years ago
Last ice age begins, 100,000 years ago

Holocene, 10,000 years ago-the present
First civilizations, 10,000 years ago

Devonian 395-345 mya
First amphibians, 350 mya

Silurian 435-395 mya
First animals live on land, 395 mya

At a glance

To see at a glance the periods covered on each page, look out for timelines like the one below throughout the book.

| Pre-Cambrian | Cambrian |

he Beginning of Life

first known life on
th is 3,200 million
rs old. Fossils of
, simple cells were
nd in cherts (a type
flint) in South Africa.
ese cells were so
all that thousands
uld have fitted
to the head
a pin.

imple cells
hown 33,000
imes their
actual size

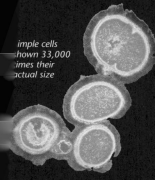

Plants lived long before the first animals.
They made oxygen, which animals breathe
to stay alive. Until there was enough oxygen,
there could be no animal life.

The first plants made oxygen under water.

Sunny cells

**200 million years after
the first known life on
Earth, tiny cells, called
blue-green bacteria, began
to use sunlight and water
to make their own food.
This process is called
photosynthesis and it is
how all plants survive.
Blue-green bacteria still
live today in the same form
as they did 3,000 mya.**

These blue-green bacteria have been magnified over 1,000 times.

INTERNET LINK

For a link to a website where you can take a tour
around an exhibit about life on Earth go to
www.usborne-quicklinks.com

Developing cells

Life developed over millions of years. The first life forms were very simple cells
but 2,400 million years later, complex, multi-celled living things began to appear.

Developed	Type of organism	Characteristics
3,200 mya	Prokaryotic cells	Very simple; produce oxygen; offspring are exact copies of themselves
1,500 mya	Eukaryotic cells	Contains specialized structures for different jobs; needs oxygen; offspring are a mixture of both parents
600 mya	Metazoa	Multi-celled organisms

Multi-celled animals

The earliest multi-celled animals can be grouped into three basic categories:

Sponges
These are the simplest multi-celled animals. They pull water through their bodies and filter it for food.

Cnidarians
These include corals, sea anemones and jellyfish. They have sack-like bodies and tentacles to direct food into their mouths.

Worm-like creatures
These animals had fluid-filled cavities inside their bodies. They are now extinct.

Fossils of jellyfish as big as truck wheels were found at Ediacara, Australia. Fossils of soft-bodied animals are rare but the shape of these jellyfish, which were stranded on a beach 670 mya, was preserved by a layer of sand before their bodies rotted.

These soft-bodied animals floated through the Pre-Cambrian waters.

Yet to come...

Here is a list of things that did not yet exist when the Cambrian period ended 550 mya (2,650 million years after the first appearance of life on Earth).

Animals with backbones

Animals with jaws or teeth

Living things on land

Amphibians

Mammals

Reptiles

Insects

Humans

Birds

These sea pens are a type of soft coral.

Shells and Skeletons

The first known shellfish lived in the Cambrian period, 570-500 mya. An enormous number of new animals with shells and skeletons appeared at this time. These creatures made good fossils, so scientists have been able to study their development.

This marella is a relative of the crab.

Shell protection

At the start of the Cambrian period, some worm-like animals began to hunt and eat other animals. They were less likely to eat creatures with shells and skeletons, so more of those creatures survived.

Common fossil

Brachiopods (lampshells) are one of the most commonly found fossils. There are about 300 species of brachiopod living in the seas today but at least 30,000 different species lived in the past.

Brachiopod shells made good fossils.

A fossil of a trilobite's protective outer skeleton.

Our first ancestors?

Chordates are a group of animals which have a stiff rod running down their body. The earliest known chordate is the Chinese cathaymyrus. Humans are also chordates, so this eel-like creature could be one of our first ancestors.

This cathaymyrus dates back 53.5 million years.

Sponges provided homes and meals for spiny worms.

Some bizarre Cambrian fossils were found in the Burgess Shale rocks in Canada. The fossils show soft-bodied creatures in great detail. In some, the animal's last meal can still be seen inside its body.

This spiky hallucigenia was found in the Burgess Shale.

The Age of Trilobites

The Cambrian period is known as "The Age of Trilobites". Trilobites were among the first arthropods – creatures with jointed legs and outer skeletons. They were usually small, but some grew up to 70cm long, which is around the length of an adult's arm.

Trilobites were the first animals to have eyes. Human beings have one lens in each eye, but some trilobites had as many as 20,000.

A close-up of a trilobite eye, made up of thousands of lenses

Trilobites are related to shrimps and lobsters.

Still here

In the Ordovician and Silurian periods (500-395 mya) yet more creatures with shells and skeletons evolved. They took the place of Cambrian animals that had died out. Some of these replacements are still around today.

The coral calendar

500 mya, a year lasted for 428 days. How do we know this? Coral grows a fresh band of skeleton every day and the size of each band depends on the season in which it was grown. Scientists are able to calculate how long a prehistoric year lasted by examining the size and number of bands on fossils of coral.

The outer layer of a coral reef

Inside, bands of skeleton grow.

The outer layer of this coral has worn away, leaving only the skeleton.

Starfish

Nautiloids

Corals

Sea anemones

Sea lilies

Sea snails

INTERNET LINK
For a link to a website where you can discover why some sea creatures developed shells go to **www.usborne-quicklinks.com**

The First Fish

Fish appeared 540 mya in what is now China. The first fish had no jaws, so ate by sucking in water and filtering out pieces of food.

Jaws

The first fish with jaws appeared during the Silurian period (435-395 mya). They are known as acanthodians, or "spiny sharks", although they were not sharks at all.

Their spiny fins made acanthodians difficult to eat.

Confirmed colour

In 1997, a fossil of a placoderm – a Silurian fish – was found to contain colour cells showing that it had a silver belly and a red back. The placoderm is the oldest ever vertebrate fossil to be found with preserved traces of skin colour.

The placoderm's skin colour may have looked like this.

The first sharks

Sharks first appeared during the Devonian period. A shark's skeleton is made up of cartilage (the same material that is in the tip of your nose).

Cartilage is lighter than bone and this helps sharks to float. Sharks and rays were probably the last major group of fish to evolve.

This early shark's body is streamlined so it can glide through the water.

Fish were the first creatures to have a backbone. Animals with a backbone are called vertebrates. Over half of the 42,000 species of vertebrates known in the world are fish.

Ostracoderms — the first animals to have backbones

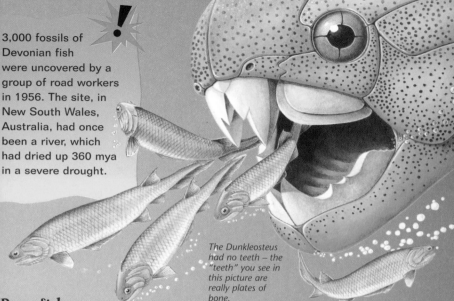

3,000 fossils of Devonian fish were uncovered by a group of road workers in 1956. The site, in New South Wales, Australia, had once been a river, which had dried up 360 mya in a severe drought.

The Dunkleosteus had no teeth – the "teeth" you see in this picture are really plates of bone.

Bony fish

As bony fish developed, they split into two groups:

Ray finned fish have delicate, fan-shaped fins supported by fine, bony rods. Most fish that are alive today are ray fins.

Fleshy finned fish have muscular fins, edged with a fringe of fine rays. These fish developed into the first land-living vertebrates.*

Ray fin

Fleshy fin

Shark-eater

The largest predator of the Devonian seas was the shark-eating Dunkleosteus. It had sharp jaws, but no teeth. Instead of scales, its body was covered with hinged plates.

INTERNET LINK
For a link to a website where you can find animations and information about prehistoric sharks go to **www.usborne-quicklinks.com**

Devonian sea monster	Length	Location of fossils	Distinctive features
Dunkleosteus	9m	Africa, Belgium, Morocco, Poland, USA	Heavily armoured; scissor-like jaws
Hyneria lindae	4m	USA	Rough scales; long, sharp teeth
Gyracanthus	2m	Australia, USA, UK	Long spine
Ctenacanthus	nearly 2m	USA, UK	Spines on fins

* See page 149

Plants on Land

For millions of years, the Earth's surface was scorched by the Sun's ultraviolet rays. Nothing could live on land. Simple plants, called algae, grew at the sea's edges, but the rest of the land was rocky and probably bare.

Gradually, a layer of gas called ozone built up around the Earth. It blocked out some of the Sun's rays, enabling plants and animals to live on land.

Plants had been on land for 300 million years before the first flower bloomed. One of the earliest flowering plants was the magnolia. It looked the same as the magnolias we see today.

Upright plants

To be able to survive on land, plants developed an outer layer to stop them from drying out and inner, woody tubes to carry water through their stems. These tubes keep the plants upright.

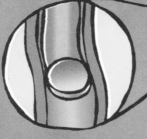

This stem has a tube inside to carry water.

Ferns grew in the hot and steamy prehistoric forests.

The first land plant

The earliest known evidence of plant life on land is a Cooksonia fossil dating back 420 million years. The Cooksonia was simply a stem with a capsule at its tip and had no leaves, roots or flowers.

Cooksonia capsules contained spores.

A modern magnolia flower

INTERNET LINK

For a link to a website where you can explore pictures and information about the Earth's oldest plants go to **www.usborne-quicklinks.com**

Making coal

Coal is made from prehistoric plants. As plants died, layers of plant material built up, forming peat. The heavy layers above squeezed water and gases out of the peat underneath, and turned it into coal.

Layers of dead plant material covered prehistoric forest floors

The deepest layers formed the coal we mine today.

Plant family history

By studying the cells of over 300 modern plants, scientists were able to make a chart to show the order in which modern plants first evolved on land. Green algae in the water evolved into the first land plants – a type of liverwort. All modern land plants are descended from these early liverworts.

Familiar plants

The hot, steamy forests and swamps of the Carboniferous period contained some types of plant that can still be found today:

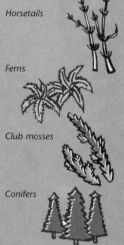

Horsetails

Ferns

Club mosses

Conifers

A modern liverwort

Spores and seeds

The earliest plants produced tiny cells, called spores. Spores were carried away by the wind or water and then grew into new plants.

During the Devonian period (395-345 mya), some plants, such as seed-ferns, began to produce seeds instead of spores. Seeds are tougher than spores and can grow in drier soil.

This fossil of a seed fern looks very similar to the ferns we see today.

Timeline of plant evolution		
		Flowering plants
		Ferns
		Mosses
		Liverworts
		Green algae
500 mya	250 mya	**Present**

Animals on Land

Once plants began to grow on land, there was food for animals to eat. The first creatures to move from water onto land were invertebrates – they did not have backbones.

The first animals to fly were insects. Some were huge. The largest insect ever to have lived was the Meganeura – a giant dragonfly that developed 280 mya.

The Meganeura had a 75cm wingspan – the same as a seagull.

Land crawlers

In the Devonian period (395-345 mya), the most common creatures on land were arthropods – animals with jointed legs and outer skeletons. Many that developed at this time are still common today:

Centipede

Millipede

Spider

Mite

Scorpion

Cockroach

Insect bites

The earliest known insect is a tiny springtail called a Rhyniella. It lived 380 mya among plants found in Rhynie, Scotland. Fossils of these plants had holes showing where the insects had fed.

Rhyniellas – the first known insects

Amber traps

Insect fossils are very rare because their bodies are so delicate. Insects can become fossilized when they are trapped in resin – a sticky liquid which oozes from pine trees. Prehistoric resin turns into a yellow stone, called amber.

A prehistoric insect trapped in amber

Air and water

About 375 mya, an animal called an Icthyostega appeared. It lived mainly in the water but could also breathe air and crawl on land. Animals that live on land but lay their eggs in the water are called amphibians.

Icthyostegas could survive on land...

...and underwater.

The Icthyostega had a strong skeleton to support its large body. Animals that live only in water do not need a strong skeleton because their bodies are supported by the water.

The Icthyostega dragged itself around by its powerful front legs.

The amphibian problem

Early amphibians had the advantage of being able to live both on land and underwater, but there were disadvantages too.

Early amphibians could:	Early amphibians could not:
Breathe air	Mate on dry land
Use their legs and backbones to move around on land	Keep their bodies warm during cold weather
Use their ears to hear sounds in the air	Keep water in their bodies to prevent them from drying out

Growing legs

Scientists believe that amphibians evolved from fleshy finned fish. These fish had lungs and large fins supported by bones and muscles. They could use their fins to push their heads above the water for brief periods. These fins probably developed into amphibian legs.

An amphibian called a Diplocaulus had a boomerang-shaped head that helped it to glide through the water. Its odd shape may have also made the creature difficult for predators to swallow.

The Diplocaulus swam using its head.

INTERNET LINK

For a link to a website where you can see how animals arrived on land go to
www.usborne-quicklinks.com

Changing World

The Earth's surface is made up of several huge pieces, called plates. The plates float on a constantly moving layer of rock. Some plates, carried by the rock, are pushed together while others are pulled apart.

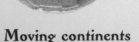

This piece of the Earth's crust is the South American plate.

Land masses on the Earth's surface move along with the plates underneath, drifting at the same speed that your fingernails grow. This movement created the seven continents we know today. They once fitted together like jigsaw pieces, but then drifted apart. This was proved by the discovery of identical plant and animal fossils on the coasts of South America and Africa.

Moving continents

Over millions of years, the movement of the Earth's plates can make the continents drift huge distances.

250 mya, the Earth's three continents collided to make one supercontinent.

By 120 mya, the supercontinent had begun to break up.

By 60 mya, the supercontinent had begun to separate into the seven continents we have today.

Changing climates

The movement of the continents means that the places we know today were very different millions of years ago.

• 450 mya, the Sahara desert was where Antarctica is now and was covered in ice.

• During the Carboniferous period (345-280 mya), Europe and Antarctica were situated on the Equator. This meant that they had very hot climates.

• 200 mya, New York was part of a large lake which was home to the earliest known gliding reptile, called Icarosaurus.

• 50 mya, London had a hot and humid climate. It was covered in swamps where crocodiles and turtles lived.

Turtle – an early Londoner

Future shocks

When the Earth's plates scrape against each other, stress builds up in between.

If the pressure becomes too great, energy is released and an earthquake occurs.

Scientists look for damage to rocks to find out where earthquakes struck in prehistoric times. This helps them work out where future earthquakes may happen.

INTERNET LINK

For a link to a website where you can see what the Earth looked like in the past and what it may look like in the future, go to **www.usborne-quicklinks.com**

In 1970, scientists discovered that only 6 mya, the Mediterranean Sea was a dry valley. When the Earth's crust moved, the Atlantic Ocean burst over the Straits of Gibraltar in a spectacular waterfall. It took over 100 years to fill the Mediterranean valley with water.

Making mountains

When two of the Earth's plates are pushed together, the land crumples up at the edges to form great stretches of mountain. The world's biggest mountain ranges were formed in this way.

Mountain range	When formed	How formed
The Appalachians	250 mya	Africa and North America collided, pushing up the sea floor.
The Ural Mountains	250 mya	Three continents collided to make one large continent, pushing up the land.
The Andes	80 mya	The Pacific Ocean floor sunk under the edge of South America, pushing up the land.
The Himalayas	40 mya (and still forming)	India collided with the Asian continent.
The Alps	15 mya	Africa moved north, pushing the Mediterranean sea floor against Europe.

The Alps began to be made 15 mya and are still forming today.

Before the Dinosaurs

Before dinosaurs appeared, the Earth was inhabited by their earliest relatives. They belonged to a group called amniotes. Amniotes reproduced using eggs containing fluid to protect the growing baby. Today, some amniotes (such as humans) house the growing baby and fluid inside their bodies. Reptiles are one of the earliest amniote groups.

Inside this egg a baby reptile grows, protected from the outside world.

Land lovers

Unlike amphibians, reptiles are able to live on land all the time. This is because they have three major adaptations to life on land that amphibians did not have.

- Scaly skin – reptiles have scaly, waterproof skin to stop their bodies from losing too much water.

- Strong legs – reptiles can lift their bodies off the ground and are able to move around easily on land.

- Eggs with shells – reptile eggs are laid on land and have a waterproof shell that protects the baby.

Sailing back

During the Permian period, a group of amniotes called synapsids developed. Some early synapsids had sails of skin on their backs that they could turn to face the Sun when they needed heat.

This synapsid's sail of skin helped to control its body temperature.

The oldest known fossil eggs in the world were laid by reptiles in the Permian Period (280-230 mya). They were the size of chickens' eggs.

New and improved

About 270 mya, synapsids began to develop longer legs that grew directly underneath their bodies. This allowed them to take bigger strides and move around faster. These new synapsids were called therapsids.

This meat-eating therapsid had long legs for extra speed.

Back to the water

Although reptiles had evolved to cope with life on land, some went back to living in the water. One of the earliest to do this was the Mesosaurus. It returned to the water during the Permian period (280-230 mya).

A Mesosaurus had long, spiky teeth which it used to trap small, shrimp-like creatures in its mouth. It may have had a fin on its tail and webbed feet to help it swim.

The Mesosaurus' feet became webbed to help it swim under water.

INTERNET LINK
To find a link to a website where you can see a therapsid hunting for food, go to
www.usbornequicklinks.com

Furry friends

By the start of the Triassic period (230 mya), a new type of therapsid, called a cynodont, had emerged. Cynodonts had slim bodies and powerful jaws lined with different types of teeth. Some probably grew fur to keep their bodies warm. By the end of the Triassic period (208 mya), furry cynodonts had developed into a completely new group of amniotes called mammals*.

This cynodont is an ancestor of mammals.

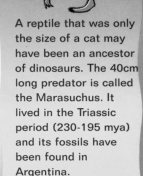

Marasuchus

A reptile that was only the size of a cat may have been an ancestor of dinosaurs. The 40cm long predator is called the Marasuchus. It lived in the Triassic period (230-195 mya) and its fossils have been found in Argentina.

*See page 164

153

Dinosaur Giants

Dinosaurs are a type of reptile. Most species died out at the end of the Cretaceous period (65 mya), but some dinosaurs are still around today. They can be seen flying through the air, swimming in the water or nesting in trees. This is because all birds are a type of dinosaur.

Great lizards

Dinosaur fossils were first studied by a British scientist called Sir Richard Owen. In 1841, he invented the name dinosaur. The name comes from the Greek *deinos*, which means fearfully great, and *sauros*, which means lizard.

deinos + sauros = fearfully great lizard!

A 30-tonne Seismosaurus

Top five dinosaur giants

The longest and heaviest land animals ever to have lived were sauropods. They appeared at the end of the Triassic period (230-208 mya). Sauropods were plant-eaters with large bodies, small heads and extremely long necks and tails.

Sauropod	Weight	Length
Amphicoelias	150 tonnes	60m
Supersaurus	55 tonnes	42m
Argentinosaurus	90 tonnes	41m
Andesaurus	12.5 tonnes	40m
Seismosaurus	30 tonnes	35m

Until around 150 years ago, no one knew that dinosaurs had existed. So when, in 1677, part of a Megalosaurus' leg bone was discovered in England, people thought that it had belonged to a giant human.

Digging up giant bones

Identity crisis

In 1979, a scientist discovered huge pieces of fossilized dinosaur bone in Colorado, USA. He thought he had discovered a new type of giant dinosaur, measuring 25-30m in length. He named it "Ultrasauros". Later, it was discovered that the bones he found may have belonged to two separate dinosaurs – a Supersaurus and a Brachiosaurus.

The "Ultrasauros" – one dinosaur or two?

Chewing trouble

Sauropods used their long necks to reach the very tops of trees. Their peg-like teeth were good for stripping leaves, but not so good for chewing. This meant they had to swallow tough leaves and twigs without having fully chewed them. They may have swallowed stones to help grind up the food in their stomachs.

Diplodocus swallowed tough leaves and twigs.

High pressure

Some sauropods held their heads high above the ground. To pump blood up the long neck to the brain, they had very large and powerful hearts. Their blood pressure needed to be three or four times as high as a human's.

INTERNET LINK
For a link to a website where you can take an interactive journey with a sauropod family go to **www.usborne-quicklinks.com**

Record-breaking body part	Belonged to...	Length (approx)	
Horn	Triceratops	1m	
Claw	Therizinosaurus	70cm	
Neck	Sauroposeidon	15m	
Head	Pentaceratops	3m	
Teeth	Gigantosaurus	15cm	

More Dinosaurs

Over 800 species of dinosaur have been found. Scientists have divided them into two groups, called lizard-hipped and bird-hipped dinosaurs. Lizard-hipped dinosaurs can be identified by their clawed feet and bird-hipped dinosaurs can be identified by their hoofed toes.

Clawed feet   *Hoofed toes*

Tall tail

The largest meat-eater that has ever lived on land was the fierce Tyrannosaurus rex. It was as long as a humpback whale (around 12.5m) and weighed as much as an African elephant (around 6 tonnes). When walking or running, it had to hold it tail high to balance the weight of its huge head.

Tyrannosaurus rex had a heavy head.

INTERNET LINK
For a link to a website where you can explore an amazing dinosaur directory go to **www.usborne-quicklinks.com**

Hadrosaurs, also called "duck-bills" because of their broad beaks, had up to 960 teeth in the sides of their jaws at any one time. New teeth grew as others wore out.

Deadliest dinosaurs

The deadliest dinosaurs lived in the Cretaceous period (145-65 mya). Most belonged to a group called dromaeosaurs. They were fast-moving meat-eaters with long claws, sharp teeth and long arms that gave them more stability and mobility when hunting.

These deadly dinosaurs included:

- Dromaeosaurus
- Deinonychus
- Microraptor
- Velociraptor
- Utahraptor

Dromaeosaurs had long arms...

...long claws...

...and very sharp teeth.

Smallest dinosaurs

Fossils of small dinosaurs are very rarely found. This is because small dinosaurs were usually eaten by bigger animals and any remaining traces are difficult to spot. The smallest dinosaurs discovered so far are:

- Saltopus – this insect-eater was 70cm long and about the size of a small cat.

Saltopus

- Compsognathus – this meat-eater was 60cm long and about the size of a chicken.

Compsognathus

- Lesothosaurus – this lizard-like dinosaur was about 1m long and ate plants.

- Microraptor – this bird-like dinosaur was 40cm long and about the size of a crow. It may have spent much of its life in trees.

Microraptor

Lesothosaurus

- Wannanosaurus – this thick-skulled dinosaur was about 60cm long and ate plants.

Wannanosaurus

The Stegosaurus had the smallest brain of any animal compared to its size. Its body was 6m long, but the "thinking" part to its brain was only the size of a walnut.

A walnut

Triceratops' three horns were useful weapons.

What's in a name?

A newly discovered dinosaur is named by the person who finds or classifies it. There are many ways to choose a dinosaur name.

Dinosaur	Reason for name
Triceratops	The three horns on its head
Andesaurus	Fossils first discovered in the Andes mountains in South America
Lambeosaurus	In honour of scientist, Lawrence Lamb
Spinosaurus	The spines on its back
Velociraptor	It could run at high speeds

Dinosaur Lifestyles

Plant-eating dinosaurs needed to defend themselves from predatory meat-eaters. They did this in a number of ways:

• The Polacanthus' weapons were spikes growing on its back and its tail was protected by bony plates.

Spiny back

• The Hypsilophodon was only about 60cm tall. It had long legs and could run quickly to escape from predators.

Long legs

• The Euoplocephalus stunned attackers with a bony club on its tail.

Tail club

• The Stegosaurus was protected by large, bony plates on its back and the spikes on its tail.

Back plates

Head bangers

The Pachycephalosaurus, or bone-headed dinosaur, had a skull up to 25cm thick. It used its skull as a battering ram when it charged, head first, at predators. The males probably also fought each other to attract a mate by proving their strength.

Pachycephalosaurus could use its head as a battering ram.

Running with dinosaurs

Scientists can estimate a dinosaur's speed by examining its body structure and footprints. The bigger dinosaurs could reach high speeds, but only for very short periods.

Dinosaur	Highest speed
Ornithomimus	70 kph
Dilophosaurus	65 kph
Velociraptor	60 kph
Triceratops	30 kph
Tyrannosaurus rex	25 kph

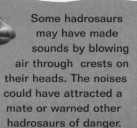

Some hadrosaurs may have made sounds by blowing air through crests on their heads. The noises could have attracted a mate or warned other hadrosaurs of danger.

Stampede!

Footprints of over 130 stampeding dinosaurs were found in Queensland, Australia. They had been running at a speed of 8kph, chased by a giant meat-eating dinosaur running at 15kph.

INTERNET LINK

For a link to a website where you can play a dinosaur survival game go to **www.usborne-quicklinks.com**

Dinosaur nursery

Hundreds of fossilized dinosaur nests, eggs, embryos and babies were found on "Egg Mountain" in Montana, USA. Each nest housed up to 26 eggs. The mountain was once home to 10,000 Maiasaura — a name which means "good mother reptile".

A fossilized "nursery" was found in Montana, USA.

NORTH AMERICA

Montana

Maiasaura eggs, nests and babies were discovered.

Animals in the Sky

Rhamphorhynchus

Around 225 mya, some reptiles developed wings. They are known as pterosaurs. They may have evolved from tree-climbing reptiles which had flaps of skin under their limbs to help them to glide from branch to branch. Pterosaurs are not dinosaurs.

An early gliding reptile

Why fly?

Scientists have many ideas about why some animals began to fly:

• To help move from place to place (by leaping or gliding)

• To free the hind legs for use as weapons

• To help escape from predators

• To reach new food sources or unused living spaces

• To help catch flying or speedy prey

The Pteranodon could swallow a fish whole while in flight.

The largest flying animal ever to have lived is a Quetzalcoatlus — a pterosaur the size of a small aircraft. Its fossils were discovered in Texas, USA.

Central heating

Normally, reptiles rely on the Sun's heat to keep their bodies warm, but pterosaurs could produce their own heat, like birds do. Some pterosaurs were covered with fur, to stop them losing too much heat through their skin.

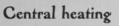
Pterodactylus

Feathered dinosaurs

Most scientists believe that birds are descended from dinosaurs and not from pterosaurs. Modern birds have similar skeletons to some meat-eating dinosaurs.

In the late 1990s, fossils of three new dinosaurs were found in China. The fossils show that they were covered in feathers, but they probably could not fly.

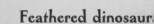
Sinosaupteryx — a feathery dinosaur.

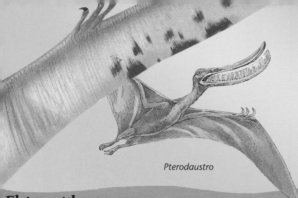

Gliders and fliers

Pterosaurs had light bones and strong muscles which helped them to fly. Those living near water or on cliffs could also glide. They may have glided to save energy so they could stay in the air longer.

Pterodaustro

Flying with pterosaurs

By the Jurassic period, 208 mya, there were several types of pterosaur. They all had big, leathery wings and long necks.

Pterosaur	Developed	Distinguishing features
Rhamphorhynchus	150-145 mya	Pointed jaws to catch fish
Pterodactylus	145 mya	Short tail to help it turn quickly in the air
Pterodaustro	125 mya	Long, curved beak; trapped tiny sea creatures between thin teeth
Pteranodon	85 mya	No teeth, swallowed fish whole
Quetzalcoatlus	70-65 mya	10m wing span

Early bird

The earliest known bird is the Archaeopteryx, which means "ancient wing". It appeared about 145 mya. Although it had feathers and wings like a bird, it also had teeth and a long, bony tail, like a dinosaur.

Although the Archaeopteryx was only the size of a crow, it was probably too heavy to take off from the ground. It may have climbed up trees and launched itself into the air from a high branch.

INTERNET LINK

For a link to a website where you can see through a pterosaur's eyes go to **www.usborne-quicklinks.com**

This early bird was a terrible flier.

Animals in the Sea

While dinosaurs were living on land, other reptiles lived in the seas. Their bodies were adapted to life under water, but they still had to come up for air every now and then.

Early sea reptiles

At the start of the Triassic period, 230 mya, there were many types of reptiles living in the sea, such as nothosaurs, placodonts and icthyosaurs.

The Mixosaurus had a fin like a shark's and a mouth like a dolphin's, but it was actually a sea reptile.

Nothosaurs had long, thin bodies that could glide smoothly through the water. They used their big, sharp teeth to catch fish.

Nothosaurs swam using their paddle-like limbs.

Ichthyosaurs had streamlined, dolphin-shaped bodies and large fins that helped them glide swiftly through the water. Their large eyes helped them to see in the dark. They may have searched for food, such as squid, fish and ammonites, in the dark depths of the oceans.

Placodonts were slow-moving reptiles that looked similar to modern turtles. They were usually 1-2m long. Some had bodies covered with plates of bone.

An armoured placodont

Ichthyosaurs flicked their tails from side to side as they swam.

Instead of laying eggs on dry land like other reptiles, ichthyosaurs gave birth to their babies under water. This meant that ichthyosaurs never had to leave the sea.

Monsters of the deep

Some of the biggest sea reptiles belonged to a group called the plesiosaurs. Like modern turtles, they swam using four flippers and probably laid their eggs on beaches.

The Liopleurodon's mouth was 3m long.

Plesiosaur	Length	Distinguishing features
Liopleurodon	12-15m	Large head and short neck; powerful jaws and teeth
Elasmosaurus	14m	Long neck that was half its length
Woolungasaurus	8-10m	Very long neck
Kronosaurus	9m	Very long head; huge, cone-shaped teeth
Muraenosaurus	6m	Long neck and wide body

Sea crocodiles

During the Jurassic period (208-145 mya), crocodiles swam in the sea. Some had flippers instead of limbs and fish-like tails to help them push themselves through the water.

Sea crocodiles could grow up to 7m long.

The pliosaur – a type of plesiosaur – could pick up the scent of other creatures in the sea by filtering water through its mouth and out of its nostrils.

This plesiosaur had a tiny head compared to its large body.

INTERNET LINKS

For a link to a website where you can go on an interactive Jurassic sea adventure go to **www.usborne-quicklinks.com**

Sea survivors

Around 65 mya, almost all sea reptiles died out. Crocodiles and turtles survived, but today, most crocodiles live in fresh water rather than in the sea. Modern-day ocean reptiles include turtles, sea snakes and marine iguanas.

Most crocodiles live in fresh water.

This modern turtle is an ocean reptile.

The Arrival of Mammals

Around 200 mya, a group of creatures called mammals began to appear. They were descended from the cynodonts* that had evolved at the start of the Triassic period.

The rat-like Megazostrodon was one of the earliest mammals.

What is a mammal?

Mammals come in many shapes and sizes, but they all have four things in common:

• They all have hair or bristles on their skin.

• They can all produce their own heat and so stay warm even when the weather is cold.

• All females feed their babies with milk.

• They all have several kinds of teeth which they use for cutting and chewing food.

Tree gliders

Some tree-climbing mammals grew flaps of skin between their legs so they could glide, much like the flying squirrels seen today.

This gliding mammal is an ancestor of the bat.

First mammal facts

The first mammals were insect-eating animals that looked like mice or shrews. For over 100 million years, until the dinosaurs died out, most mammals stayed very small.

Mammal	Developed (period)	Length	Distinguishing features
Megazostrodon	Late Triassic	10cm	Long tail, body and snout
Jeholodens	Middle Cretaceous	13cm	Grasping hands; large eyes
Deltatheridium	Late Cretaceous	15cm	Pouch; sharp teeth
Zalambdalestes	Late Cretaceous	20cm	Upturned snout; interlocking teeth

Egg-layers

The first mammals probably all laid eggs, like their reptile relatives did. However, unlike reptiles, mammals fed their young with milk. Today, mammals that lay eggs are called monotremes. The spiny anteater and duck-billed platypus are both monotremes.

These modern mammals are unusual because they lay eggs.

Spiny anteater

Duck-billed platypus

INTERNET LINK
For a link to a website where you can go to an early mammal zoo go to www.usborne-quicklinks.com

Baby on board

Around 100 mya, some mammals began to give birth to live young instead of laying eggs. The babies crawled up into a pouch on their mother's stomach and continued to grow there. Today, most mammals with pouches are called marsupials.

A few million years after marsupials appeared, placental mammals evolved. Placental females keep their babies inside their bodies until the babies are large enough to survive on their own. Most mammals alive today are placentals.

In times of drought, some marsupials can delay giving birth until the climate improves. The embryo inside the mother's body stops growing. When the weather improves, the embryo begins to grow again and eventually grows big enough to move to its mother's pouch.

This modern kangaroo is a marsupial – babies develop in the mother's pouch.

This modern elephant is a placental – babies develop in the mother's body.

More Mammals

After the dinosaurs died out around 65 mya, life became less dangerous for mammals. They began to explore new places to live and to eat a wide range of foods. A huge variety of mammals evolved and spread out all over the world.

An early bat

Meat-eaters

The first meat-eating mammals were called creodonts. They had small brains, short legs and flat feet.

Creodont

Early mammals came in all shapes and sizes.

Gradually, a new group of meat-eaters evolved that were fast-moving, powerful and cunning. These mammals, known as carnivores, had excellent hearing and eyesight and a strong sense of smell.

An early antelope

Plant-eaters

The earliest plant-eating mammals were slow-moving creatures with small brains. They wandered through forests nibbling leaves and plants.

Indricotherium snacking on a tree top

Modern cats and dogs are descended from an early type of carnivore that only ate insects. They lived around 60-65 mya and looked similar to the civets that are seen today.

An ancient relative of cats and dogs

The first deer, cattle, sheep and antelope had all appeared by 25 mya. They roamed over the grasslands in herds. Some of them developed long legs to help them run quickly and horns or antlers which they used to fight off attackers.

INTERNET LINK

For a link to a website where you can play a mammal survival game go to **www.usborne-quicklinks.com**

Horse history

The first horses appeared around 50 mya, living in the rainforests of Europe and North America.

• 50 mya, horses were only the size of cats and were sometimes attacked by vicious giant birds.

• By 35 mya, horses had grown longer legs and stronger teeth.

• By 10 mya, horses had grown to the size of small ponies. They lived in herds on the open plains.

• Around 5 mya, a new kind of horse, called Equus, appeared. Equus is the only kind of horse we see today.

Up until 2 mya, South America was not joined to North America. It had been separate for 60 million years. In that time, many mammals unknown in the rest of the world developed in South America. One such mammal was the giant, armadillo-like Glyptodon.

The Glyptodon was as big as a car.

Elephant ancestors

The earliest ancestors of today's elephants were long, pig-like animals that lived in African swamps 40 mya. They spent most of their lives wallowing in water.

An early, pig-like elephant

By 30 mya, elephants had developed short trunks and curved tusks.

By 10 mya, some elephants had spade-like teeth while others had backward-curving tusks.

About 5 mya, a new kind of elephant, called Stegodon, appeared. They looked very similar to today's elephants.

Short tusks and trunk, 30 mya

Backward-curved tusks, 20 mya

Spade-like teeth, 10 mya

Long tusks and trunk, 5 mya

Pliocene

167

Monster Mammals

Many giant mammals lived in the Pleistocene period (2 mya-10,000 years ago). However, the Uintatherium was one of the earliest giant mammals, having already become extinct by the end of the Eocene period, 38 mya.

The Uintatherium was a plant-eater that weighed over 2 tonnes.

!

The Megatherium – a Pleistocene mammal – was almost as big as a double-decker bus. Its claws were so huge that it could not put its feet flat on the ground and had to walk on the sides of its feet.

Megatherium walked on the sides of its feet.

Caving in

Fossils of some of the largest land mammals of the Pleistocene period were all found in one hole in the ground. The animals had fallen down the hole in Devon, England, 12,000 years ago. Fossils found included the remains of:

Bison

Elephants

Deer

Bears

Hippopotamuses

Lions

Rhinoceroses

Largest in prehistory	Name	Lived (period)
Sea mammal	Basilosaurus (20m long)	Eocene
Land mammal	Paraceratherium (8m tall, 11m long)	Oligocene
Carnivorous mammal	Megistotherium (6m long, weighed 900kg)	Miocene
Marsupial	Diprotodon (3m long, 2m tall)	Pleistocene
Sabre-toothed tiger	Smilodon (7.5m long, weighed 200kg)	Pleistocene
Mammoth	Imperial mammoth (4.5m tall)	Pleistocene

Smilodon

Giant ancestors

Many mammals living today are descended from giant mammals that lived in the Pleistocene period.

• The Procoptodon was the largest kangaroo ever known. It was three times taller and heavier than the biggest of today's kangaroos.

Procoptodon

• The Gigantopithecus was a great ape that was twice as tall and twice as heavy as a modern male gorilla.

Gigantopithecus lived on the forest floor as it was too heavy to climb trees.

• The Glyptodon was an armadillo-like creature the size of a small car.

• The cave bear was a powerful animal that weighed 1 tonne.

Cave bear

• The giant beaver was as long and heavy as a modern polar bear with a tail measuring 0.5m.

INTERNET LINK
For a link to a website where you can find pictures, movies and fact files about the monster mammals of the last ice age go to **www.usborne-quicklinks.com**

• The Megaceros was the biggest deer ever known. It was as tall as two men. The male's antlers had the widest span of any known animal. They were 3m wide and weighed 50kg.

• The cave lion was the biggest lion ever known. It could grow up to twice as long as today's African lions.

The biggest prehistoric mammals lived on the largest continents – North America and Asia. They were so huge that they had to live in large, open spaces to avoid overcrowding.

Woolly mammoths flourished in North America during the last ice age.

• The woolly rhino was twice as heavy as a modern black rhino. Its main horn was 1m long.

The woolly rhino used its horn to dig up food.

Ice Ages

Several times in the Earth's past, large parts of the world have been buried under thick sheets of ice. Each time, the ice has stayed frozen for thousands of years. These long, freezing periods are known as ice ages.

The Earth during the last ice age

Area covered in ice

Frozen lands where animals could live

The last ice age

The last ice age began 100,000 years ago and ended 10,000 years ago. At its peak, around 21,000 years ago, thick masses of ice covered much of North America, Europe and Asia. Almost one third of the Earth's land surface was covered by ice.

INTERNET LINK
For a link to a website where you can travel back in time to the last ice age go to **www.usborne-quicklinks.com**

Freezing reasons

The exact reasons why ice ages occur are not fully known, but there are likely to be a number of causes, such as:

• the changes in ocean circulation

• the position of the continents

• the amount of heat from the Sun trapped in the Earth's atmosphere

• the concentration of gases in the Earth's atmosphere

Bridging the gap

As sea water turned to ice in the last ice age, the world's sea level lowered at a rate of 12m every 1,000 years. This created land bridges between places that had been separated by sea. Animals could then migrate to other continents. Bridges were created between Britain and the rest of Europe, Alaska and Siberia, and Africa and Europe.

Falling sea levels exposed areas of land that had been under water.

170

Living on the edge

At the start of the last ice age, many animals moved to warmer areas but some stayed in the frozen lands, called tundra, near the edge of the ice sheets. The animals that lived there became adapted to life in a cold environment.

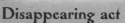

The woolly rhinoceros had a useful horn.

Animal	Adaptation
Woolly mammoth	Body covered with thick hair to keep it warm
Arctic hare	Body covered with white fur to help it hide in the snow
Woolly rhinoceros	Used its horn to brush aside snow to reach underlying vegetation
Cave bear	Sheltered in caves during the harsh winters

Ice traps

Sometimes animals fell into swamps which later froze solid. The animals' bodies were trapped in ice and could not rot away, remaining preserved for thousands of years. In the last 300 years, 4,700 frozen mammoths have been found in the icy ground of Siberia, in northern Russia.

 A frozen mammoth found in 1900 in Siberia, still had 14kg of undigested food in its stomach. The mammoth was so well preserved 30,000 years after being frozen, that people were able to eat some of its meat.

Disappearing act

At the end of the last ice age, around 10,000 years ago, many animals died out. No one knows exactly why this happened, but one reason might have been the change in the weather, which caused the ice sheets to melt.

Some animals, such as mammoths, were hunted by early humans, and this could be another reason why they disappeared.

This frozen baby mammoth was found in Siberia in 1977.

Early human hunters may have caused the extinction of the mammoths.

171

Extinction

At different times in the Earth's past, groups of animals and plants have died out suddenly. Listed below are examples of species that died out during major extinctions at the end of six prehistoric periods:

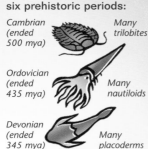

Cambrian
(ended
500 mya)
Many
trilobites

Ordovician
(ended
435 mya)
Many
nautiloids

Devonian
(ended
345 mya)
Many
placoderms

Permian
(ended
230 mya)
Most
reptiles

Triassic
(ended
208 mya)
Many
sponges

Cretaceous
(ended
65 mya)

All dinosaurs
except birds

Biggest extinction

At the end of the Permian period, 230 mya, many plants and animals suddenly died out. It was the biggest mass extinction the world has ever known and caused the death of:

- 29% of insect species

- 67% of amphibian species

- 78% of reptile species

- Most of the land plants

All these species died out over a period of just one million years.

The Cretaceous extinction wiped out most of the dinosaurs.

About 99% of all plant and animal species that have ever lived are now extinct. There are about five million species living today, but if no species had ever become extinct, there would be 980 million.

Minor extinctions

Since the last major extinction, about 65 mya, there have been many minor extinctions. Over the last 2.5 million years, various creatures have become extinct, from large mammals to small molluscs. The most serious mammal extinction happened 10,000 years ago, at the end of the last ice age.*

Mammoths died out at the end of the last ice age.

Explaining extinction

Scientists have four main explanations for why mass extinctions occur:

The Asteroid Theory – a huge asteroid hits the Earth, producing a dust cloud that blocks out all sunlight. It may also cause earthquakes and tidal waves.

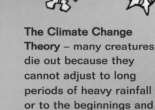

The Climate Change Theory – many creatures die out because they cannot adjust to long periods of heavy rainfall or to the beginnings and ends of ice ages.

The Volcano Theory – rock pours out from the Earth's crust, throwing up dust and smoke that blocks out all sunlight and acid that poisons the oceans.

The Sea Level Change Theory – many creatures die out because they cannot adjust to the disruption of their habitats caused by changes in sea level.

Most animals that weighed over 10kg died at the end of the Cretaceous period. But all small insects and some small birds, lizards and sea creatures survived. Why most of the larger animals died out and the smaller ones didn't, is a mystery.

The dragonfly is a survivor.

Dinosaur death

Many other reasons have been suggested for why the dinosaurs died out, including:

- diseases
- over-eating
- infertility
- poisonous plants
- their eggs eaten by birds or mammals.

INTERNET LINK
For a link to a website where you can find information about extinction go to **www.usborne-quicklinks.com**

Period of extinction	Probable causes
Cambrian	Climate change, Sea level change
Ordovician	Climate change, Sea level change
Devonian	Climate change
Permian	Asteroid, Volcano, Climate change, Sea level change
Triassic	Climate change
Cretaceous	Asteroid, Volcano

Our Ancestors

Over millions of years, a group of mammals called primates developed into the first human beings. The earliest primates were small, squirrel-like creatures that scurried around in trees.

This Plesiadapis is one of your early relatives.

Shrinking snouts

Most early primates had long noses, or snouts, for sniffing out food. Some later primates relied on their eyes instead of their noses to find food, so their snouts gradually became shorter.

From long snout to stubby nose

Apes and monkeys

The first monkeys and apes evolved from primates around 30 mya. The earliest monkeys were expert tree-climbers and some developed long tails for grasping branches. Apes were bigger and stronger than monkeys. They had broad chests and strong arms which helped them to swing from tree to tree.

Two early apes grooming

Almost human

By 14 mya, some primates had developed many human-like features:

• Their eyesight developed so that they could see shapes and judge distances better.

• They began to walk on two feet instead of walking on all fours.

• Their paws had developed into fingers and toes with sensitive tips.

• They lived in groups and looked after each other, spending a long time showing their children how to survive.

The first humans to discover fire probably could not light fires for themselves. They may have found fires that had started when lightning struck dry grass and then carried a burning branch away to a cave or camp. They could have kept the same fire burning for days, or even weeks.

INTERNET LINK
For a link to a website where you can journey through human evolution go to **www.usborne-quicklinks.com**

Walking upright

Primates that walk upright (including humans) are called hominids. The most famous set of hominid bones is an Australopithecus skeleton from Ethiopia. The skeleton has been named "Lucy".

A group of Australopithecus – the earliest hominids – using sticks to hunt termites.

Name of primate	Lived	Average size	Major achievement
Sivapithecus	14-8 mya	90 cm tall, weighed 12kg	This early ape could walk short distances on two feet and used its hands to carry food.
Australopithecus	5-1.5 mya	1.2m tall weighed 23kg	This man-ape was the first primate to walk upright.
Homo habilis	2-1.5 mya	1.5m tall weighed 45kg	This earliest human began making stone tools to strip meat from animal carcasses.
Homo erectus	1.5 mya-200,000 years ago	1.6m tall weighed 60kg	This upright man hunted large animals and used fire for cooking and keeping warm.
Homo sapiens neanderthalensis	200,000-40,000 years ago	1.7m tall weighed 70kg	This Neanderthal man made clothes and shelters from animal skins.
Homo sapiens sapiens	40,000 years ago-the present	1.8m tall weighs 70kg	This modern man developed a spoken language to communicate with others.

Sivapithecus used its hands to carry food.

Homo habilis made stone tools.

Homo erectus used fur to make clothes.

Pliocene   Pleistocene

Famous Finds

Scientists have been finding fossils of early humans all over the world for over a hundred years. Many important fossils have been found around the Great Rift Valley in Africa. Early human fossils were first found there in 1958 and discoveries are still being made there today.

The red mark on this map of Africa shows where the Great Rift Valley lies.

So far, Africa is the only continent where our earliest human ancestors (Australopithecus and Homo habilis) have been discovered.

The skull of one of our African ancestors

Amazing trace fossils were found here in South Africa. Follow the footprints to find out more...

INTERNET LINK

For a link to a website where you can follow a timeline of human fossil discovery go to **www.usborne-quicklinks.com**

Fossil footprints

In 1997, scientists discovered a trail of fossilized footprints on the shore of a South African lagoon. They are thought to have been left by a Homo sapiens sapiens 117,000 years ago. The footprints are the earliest known trace fossils of modern human beings.

The biggest hoax in the history of fossil finds took place in 1912, when a supposedly human fossil was found in a gravel pit in Piltdown, England. The fossil came to be known as "Piltdown Man". After 40 years of fame, it was found to be a fake. The skull's jaw was from a 500 year old orang-utan.

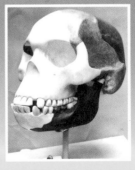

The Piltdown Man's skull was not entirely human.

Oldest inhabitants

• The oldest Australian human fossils are bones belonging to a 60,000 year old Neanderthal found in Southeastern Australia. It was nicknamed "Mungo Man".

Mungo Man may have looked like this.

• The oldest Asian human fossil is the skull of a 2 million year-old Homo erectus. It was nicknamed "Java Man".

• The oldest European human fossils are two skulls that probably date back over 1.5 million years, found in the former Republic of Georgia.

• The oldest American human fossil is an 11,500 year-old skull found in Brazil. It was nicknamed "Luiza".

• The oldest British human fossils are a limb bone and tooth that belonged to a 500,000 year-old Homo erectus that was nicknamed "Boxgrove Man".

Fossils found	When	Where
The first Homo erectus bones to be discovered	1891	Java
Neanderthal skeleton	1908	France
14 skullcaps, several facial, jaw and limb bones, and the teeth of 40 Homo erectus individuals	1927	China
A 2 million year old Homo erectus child's skull	1936	Java
Nine skeletons in a Neanderthal burial site	1957	Iraq
A 3 million year old Australopithecus skeleton that came to be known as "Lucy"	1974	Ethiopia
An Australopithecus skeleton – the most complete skeleton ever found.	1998	South Africa
A 3.5 million year old skull of a new type of man-ape, given the name Kenyanthropus platyops	2001	Kenya
A 7 million year old skull of a possible hominid, given the name Sahelanthropus tchadensis	2002	Chad

This Neanderthal was buried with flowers, tools and bones.

His remains were found in a Neanderthal burial site in Iraq.

Dragon bones

Local people around Choukoutien in China found pieces of bone in caves near their village. They called them "dragon bones" and used them in herbal remedies. In 1927, some of the bones were found to belong to a new species of Homo erectus that lived in the area 500,000-250,000 years ago. It came to be known as "Peking Man".

Peking Man was mistaken for a dragon.

Finding Food

The first modern people hunted animals and gathered plants to eat. They moved from place to place in search of food. People who live like this are called hunter-gatherers.

Some hunters used slings to swing rocks round...

...and then let them go, hoping to hit a bird.

Herd followers

Hunter-gatherers had to follow the herds of wild animals they hunted. Some European and Asian tribes followed herds of animals, such as reindeer and bison, all year round. The animals led them to new places.

Hunters followed herds of bison.

Scientists once thought that our ancestors were cannibals. They found fossils of Homo erectus skulls that were broken as if to take out the brains, and bones, smashed for the marrow inside. It was thought that humans had eaten the brains and marrow as part of a ritual, but it is now believed that the injuries were caused by cave bears.

Broken skulls caused confusion about cannibals.

INTERNET LINK

For a link to a website where you can become a hunter-gatherer go to **www.usborne-quicklinks.com**

The spear is attached to a spur sticking out of the spear-thrower.

Mammoth hunters

During the last ice age, tribes living on the frozen plains of Eastern Europe became experts at hunting mammoths. They used a weapon called a spear-thrower, which allowed them to attack mammoths from a safe distance.

The hunter grips onto the spear-thrower and hurls the spear forward.

Settling down

Around 10,000 years ago, the last ice age came to an end. Forests began to grow where ice had been. Tribes of people found places where they could hunt, catch fish and grow plants all year round.

Early farmers discovered how to sow seeds...

...and reaped the rewards when harvest time came.

Domestic changes

Plants and animals grown and bred by people are described as domesticated. Over time, domesticated species change from their wild ancestors.

The horse in this Pleistocene carving must be domesticated because it is wearing a harness.

Plant	First domesticated	Place
Wheat	10,000 years ago	Iraq
Barley	10,000 years ago	Turkey
Rice	8,000 years ago	Thailand
Corn	7,500 years ago	Mexico
Potatoes	4,000 years ago	Argentina

Animal	First domesticated	Place
Sheep	10,000 years ago	Iraq
Pig	9,000 years ago	Iran
Cattle	8,000 years ago	Turkey
Camel	5,000 years ago	Saudi Arabia
Horse	5,000 years ago	Russia

Hunter-gatherer's menu

Fresh oysters
Raw seagull eggs

Elephant steak
Roast rhino rump
Roast camel hump

served with leaves, roots, berries, fruit

Mammoth Hunter's Menu

Mixed salad of shellfish

Woolly mammoth steak
Roast reindeer leg
wild boar chop
eggs, roots and tubers

Fruit and maple sap

Early Farmer's Menu

Bread and Olives

Sliced Goose breast
Roast leg of mutton
Stewed beef, peas, lentils and onions

Dates Apples Grapes

179

Making Things

Human prehistory is divided into Ages, according to the tools early people made at the time. Tools developed at different times in different places. For example, the Neolithic Age began 10,000 years ago in the Middle East, but only reached Britain 6,000 years ago.

Stone hand-axe

Harpoons made from bone and wood

Wooden ladle

Clay pot

Periods of the Stone Age

The Stone Age is the earliest period in human prehistory, when people made tools and weapons only out of stone and bone. It is divided into five periods:

Period	Began (years ago)	Type of human	Tools invented
Lower Palaeolithic	600,000	Homo erectus	Hand-axes
Middle Palaeolithic	220,000	Neanderthal	Flake tools (for cutting)
Upper Palaeolithic	35,000	Homo sapiens	Harpoons, knives
Mesolithic	12,000	Homo sapiens	Fish hooks, arrow heads, combs, needles, boats
Neolithic	10,000	Homo sapiens	Daggers, ladles, pots

! Skis made during the Upper Palaeolithic were found in Russia. They were made from bone and decorated with an elk-head design.

Made from mammoths

During the last ice age, tribes of mammoth-hunters made almost everything they needed from mammoths bodies. They made tents, clothes, weapons and even musical instruments out of mammoth bones and skins.

Hunters used mammoth bones and animal fur to make huts.

The earliest...

...cloth
Pieces of the oldest known cloth were found in Israel. They are 9,000 years old and have 11 different patterns.

...musical instruments
Flutes and whistles were used 20,000 years ago, either to make music or as signals during hunts. Flutes were made of bird and bear bones, and whistles from the toe bones of deer.

...clothes
A 37,000 year-old body was found in the frozen soil of Siberia, wearing a shirt and trousers made from animal skins.

...sails
Sailing boats were first used in the Middle East 5,000 years ago.

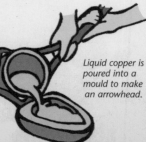

The first flutes and whistles were made from animal bones.

Early clothes were made from skins and stitched with thongs.

INTERNET LINK
For a link to a website where you can find out about Stone Age hand-axes go to **www.usborne-quicklinks.com**

The Metal Ages

For 98% of the time human beings have been on Earth, they have lived in the Stone Ages, using stone, wood and bone tools. They first learned to make tools from metal about 9,000 years ago.

Liquid copper is poured into a mould to make an arrowhead.

The oldest known wheel is about 5,500 years old. It was found in the Middle East. The first wheels were made in three stages:

1. A log was cut into rectangular sections.

2. Three rounded pieces were carved out of each section.

3. The three pieces were fixed together to make a wheel.

Age:	Began Middle East:	Began Europe:
Copper	9,000 years ago	5,000 years ago
Bronze	6,000 years ago	5,000 years ago
Iron	2,900 years ago	2,600 years ago

Building Things

In Europe, prehistoric people built huge mounds of earth and stones, called barrows, over graves. The largest one is Silbury Hill in England. It is 40m high and it covers an area of 20,000m squared. About 670,000 tonnes of chalky earth were moved to make the barrow. It would have taken the equivalent of 3,700 men 600 days to build.

Standing stones

About 4,500 years ago, prehistoric people set up large standing stones, called menhirs. Today, 3,000 menhirs still stand in Carnac, France. They form parallel lines which stretch for 6km. No one knows why the stones were put there.

One of the biggest menhirs (now broken) was about 20m high – over three times as tall as a giraffe – and weighed roughly 350 tonnes. It can be found at Locmariaquer, France.

This person is buried under a barrow.

The Celtic word menhir means "long stone".

Mystery monument

Over 4,000 years ago, a stone monument was built on Salisbury Plain, England. Who built it and why remains a mystery. The monument is called Stonehenge.

Stonehenge took 1,700 years to build. The upright stones, each weighing over 50 tonnes, were moved from 40km away. The stones for the cross pieces came from Wales, 220km away. It would have taken at least 1,000 men to drag each stone.

Nobody knows who built Stonehenge or why.

Stones were dragged along on rollers

Stonehenge would have looked like this when it was first built.

First shelters

Branch and skin tents were temporary shelters.

The first shelters were made by hunter-gatherers 40,000 years ago. They were tent-like constructions made from branches and animal skins. The shelters were only temporary because hunter-gatherers moved from place to place to find food.

INTERNET LINK
For a link to a website where you can take a tour round an ancient Turkish village go to
www.usborne-quicklinks.com

Farming villages

Once people knew how to farm they no longer needed to move around to hunt for food. They began to settle down in villages, making houses from clay bricks. Early villages were enclosed by high clay walls for protection against wild animals.

A busy farming village

Woven walls

The early Greeks built houses out of wattle and daub – sticks woven together and plastered over with mud. The roofs were thatched with grass and there was a hole in the top through which smoke could escape.

A stick framework, covered with mud

Village	Country	Built (approx. years ago)
Jericho	Jordan	10,000
Çatal Hüyük	Turkey	8,500
Dimini	Greece	7,000
Pan P'o Ts'un	China	7,000
Vinca	Serbia	7,000

Close quarters

The houses of the prehistoric Turkish village of Çatal Hüyük were closely packed together. There were no streets, but people could move from house to house by climbing ladders that hung from the roofs.

Çatal Hüyük

183

Artists and Writers

Early cave paintings show mostly animals such as bison, deer, horses and mammoths. The painters may have believed that the pictures would help them catch the animals they hunted.

Powder paints

Cave-painters made paints from minerals ground into powder. Red, yellow and brown paint was made from ochre (a mineral found in clay) and black was made from charcoal. The powder was mixed with water or fat, and painted with brushes or pads of animal fur.

This man is making brown paint from ochre.

The paint is brushed onto a cave wall to create a picture of a horse.

This horse can be seen today in the Lascaux Caves in France.

INTERNET LINK

For a link to a website where you can see prehistoric art from around the world go to **www.usborne-quicklinks.com**

!

When out hunting, prehistoric men often took carved images of very fat and pregnant women with them. The statues, made out of stone or ivory, symbolized health and fertility. They may have carried the statues to bring them good luck in their search for food.

This fat woman may have been a good luck charm.

Strung together

Early people made necklaces by stringing together animal teeth, stones, shells, fishbones and pieces of eggshell. These were probably worn for religious ceremonies and tribe leaders may have had their own special necklaces.

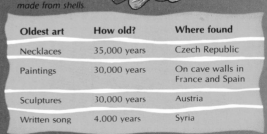

The beads on this necklace are made from shells.

Oldest art	How old?	Where found
Necklaces	35,000 years	Czech Republic
Paintings	30,000 years	On cave walls in France and Spain
Sculptures	30,000 years	Austria
Written song	4,000 years	Syria

Where writing began	When writing began
Iraq	5,500 years ago
Egypt	5,000 years ago
Indus Valley	4,600 years ago
Crete	4,000 years ago
China	3,500 years ago

This bone is engraved with the first known example of Chinese writing.

Symbols from ancient Indus Valley writing

Writing in clay

The first words were written about 5,500 years ago in Iraq. There were no separate letters; each word was a picture of an object. They were scratched onto wet clay tablets which were then dried.

Later, writers used a wedge-shaped stick to mark the clay. This writing is called cuneiform (from the Latin word for "wedge-shaped"). It stood for sounds as well as objects.

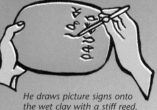

Writing from Crete, 4000 years ago

This man is flattening out clay to make tablets.

He draws picture signs onto the wet clay with a stiff reed.

Cuneiform writing on clay tablets.

The picture signs in hieroglyphics (ancient Egyptian writing) can be written from left to right or right to left. The way the pictures of men or animals are facing show which way the message should be read.

This is read from left to right.

This is read from right to left.

For the record

30,000 year-old bones provide the oldest evidence of record-keeping. The bones, found in Cromagnon, France, were engraved with a series of lines. Prehistoric people may have engraved them to record the cycle of the moon, or perhaps the number of animals killed in a hunt.

Prehistoric Survivors

Some plants and animals have remained relatively unchanged for millions of years. Studying these living fossils can help scientists understand what prehistoric plants and animals looked like and how they lived.

Nautilus

Permanent plants

Gingko – this tree has survived almost unchanged for the last 195 million years.

Gingko leaves may have been eaten by dinosaurs.

Metasequoia – this pine tree (also called Dawn Redwood) first grew on Earth 100 mya.

Cycad – this spiky plant has a fossil record 280 million years old.

Magnolia – the first magnolia trees grew 120 mya. They produced some of the first flowers.

Magnolia – an early flower

Monkey puzzle – this tree has a fossil record that dates back 250 million years.

Keep crawling

Cockroach – the first cockroach appeared on Earth 345 mya.

Cockroaches – prehistoric pests

Silverfish – this insect has remained unchanged for 395 million years.

Silverfish

Velvet worm – this caterpillar-like animal lives in the rainforest. Its ancestors crawled on the sea-floor 500 mya.

Still swimming

Nautilus – found in the Indian Ocean, this sea animal first appeared on Earth 50 mya.

Horseshoe crab – found along the Atlantic coast of the USA, this sea creature first lived on Earth 300 mya.

Australian lungfish – this fish has been on Earth for 225 million years.

Crocodile – this reptile's fossil record dates back 200 million years.

Turtle – the first turtle appeared 275 mya.

Lingula – this lampshell has one of the longest fossil records of any animal, dating back 570 million years.

Lingulas were among the first sea creatures.

INTERNET LINK
For a link to a website where you can find pictures and profiles of living fossils go to **www.usborne-quicklinks.com**

Back to life

Some plants and animals alive today were once believed to have been extinct for millions of years, only to be found alive in remote parts of the world.

In 1994, an unusual pine tree was found growing in an Australian National Park. The tree, which came to be known as the Wollemi Pine, was thought to have died out 65 mya. It is now one of the world's rarest species with only 43 adult trees known.

Coelacanth

Odd-looking, blue fish were sometimes caught off the coast of Madagascar. Locals used their skin as sandpaper. In 1938 one of the fish was identified by scientists to be a coelacanth – a creature thought to have been extinct for 70 million years.

A modern Wollemi Pine leaf with its fossil ancestors.

Okapis were thought to be extinct mammals that had evolved into horses 30 mya. Then, in 1900, okapis were discovered alive and well in Africa.

Okapis are very shy and are hard to spot in the wild.

Some people believe that there is a prehistoric monster still living in Loch Ness, Scotland. There have even been sightings of a long-necked creature in the loch. Some think that it might be a type of plesiosaur that first appeared on Earth 60 mya.

Survival tips

Most species of living fossil have survived with little change through periods of severe climate change and mass extinction. Some animals have achieved this by being able to:

• live anywhere – horseshoe crabs and cockroaches can survive extreme temperatures.

Horseshoe crab

• go without food – horseshoe crabs can go for a full year without eating.

• eat anything – cockroaches and crocodiles can eat a wide variety of food.

• heal quickly – crocodiles are tough creatures that can survive serious injuries.

Crocodiles are as tough as they look.

Dinosaurs and Prehistory Quiz

So, now you've dug up lots of prehistoric facts, how many of them can you remember? Do you know your trilobites from your tyrannosaurs? Take our quiz to find out how much of an expert you really are...

Answers on page 192

1 The Earth formed:

A 3,500 mya

B 4,200 mya

C 4,600 mya

D 5,100 mya

(See page 135)

2 Which of these isn't a type of fossil?

A body

B culinary

C molecular

D trace

(See page 136)

3 Which bacteria started to make their own food 3,000 mya?

A red-orange

B purple-pink

C blue-green

D yellow-brown

(See page 140)

4 The first animals to have eyes were:

A sea snails

B starfish

C marellas

D trilobites

(See page 143)

5 Acanthodians were difficult to eat because:

A they tasted horrible

B they had slimy skin

C they had spiny fins

D they were poisonous

(See page 144)

6 Coal is formed from:

A prehistoric plants

B prehistoric fish

C prehistoric reptiles

D prehistoric mammals

(See page 147)

7 What type of dinosaurs had crests on their heads?

A hadrosaurs

B tyrannosaurs

C dromaeosaurs

D sauropods

(See page 159)

8 Earth's surface is made up of huge pieces called:

A slabs

B squares

C bowls

D plates

(See page 150)

9 What can reptiles do that amphibians can't?

A swim in water

B walk on land

C lay eggs with waterproof shells

D produce their own heat

(See pages 149 and 152)

10 By the end of the Triassic period, furry cynodonts had developed into:

A birds

B mammals

C dinosaurs

D insects

(See page 153)

11 The longest and heaviest land animals ever were:

A hadrosaurs

B sauropods

C dromaeosaurs

D therapsids

(See page 154)

12 The two groups of dinosaurs are:

A lizard-hipped and bird-hipped

B bird-hipped and snake-hipped

C lizard-hipped and mammal-hipped

D snake-hipped and mammal-hipped

(See page 156)

13 Euoplocephalus defended itself from predators by:

A charging at them with its bony head

B sticking them with the spikes on its back

C frightening them away by making loud noises

D swinging the bony club on its tail at them

(See page 158)

14 Quetzalcoatlus is a record breaker because it is the:

A largest sea animal ever known

B largest flying animal ever known

C fastest land animal ever known

D tallest land animal ever known

(See page 160)

15 Ichthyosaurs:

A laid eggs on land

B laid eggs in water

C gave birth to live babies on land

D gave birth to live babies underwater

(See page 162)

16 The dinosaur with the biggest head was the:

A Pentaceratops

B Gigantasaurus

C Triceratops

D Therizinosaurus

(See page 155)

17 Life become less dangerous for mammals 65 mya because:

A they grew bigger

B they learned how to defend themselves

C dinosaurs died out

D poisonous plants died out

(See page 166)

18 The biggest deer ever known was the:

A Glyptodon

B Gigantopithecus

C Megaceros

D Procoptodon

(See page 169)

19 During the last ice age, which animal was covered with white fur to help it hide in the snow?

A Woolly mammoth

B Cave bear

C Woolly rhinoceros

D Arctic hare

(See page 171)

20 What percentage of reptile species became extinct at the end of the Permian period, 230 mya?

A 78%

B 64%

C 48%

D 35%

(See page 172)

21 The 3 million year-old Ethiopian Australopithecus skeleton found in 1974 was given the name:

A Mandy

B Suzy

C Wendy

D Lucy

(See page 177)

22 "Mungo Man" is the name given to the oldest:

A Asian human fossil

B European human fossil

C African human fossil

D Australian human fossil

(See page 177)

23 The first animals to fly were:

A birds

B bats

C insects

D fish

(See page 148)

24 Plants and animals grown and bred by people are described as:

A castigated

B sophisticated

C domesticated

D dessicated

(See page 179)

25 Humans learned to make tools from metal:

A 18,000 years ago

B 15,000 years ago

C 9,000 years ago

D 6,000 years ago

(See page 181)

26 "Menhir" means:

A tall building

B long stone

C big hill

D wide mound

(See page 182)

27 Prehistoric cave-painters made black paint from:

A charcoal

B mud

C leaves

D soil

(See page 184)

28 Which of these animals wasn't an early mammal?

A Megazostrodon

B Saltopus

C Deltatheridium

D Zalambdalestes

(See pages 157 and 164)

29 The animals with the longest fossil record is the:

A cockroach

B lingula

C silverfish

D crocodile

(See page 186)

30 The last ice age ended:

A 10,000 years ago

B 21,000 years ago

C 30,000 years ago

D 100,000 years ago

(See page 170)

Glossary

algae Simple plants that have no roots or leaves, ranging in size from one-celled plankton to giant seaweed.

amniotes A group of animals that reproduce using eggs that contain fluid to protect the growing embryo.

amphibians A group of animals that can live both on land and in water.

ancestor An animal or plant that is directly related to another at a later point in time.

arthropods A group of animals with jointed legs and outer skeletons.

asteroid A rocky object, smaller than a moon, that circles the Sun.

atmosphere The mixture of gases that surrounds a planet, such as the air around Earth.

bacteria Very tiny living things that live in the air, water and ground and in plants and animals.

barrow A prehistoric mound of earth and stones built over graves.

cannibal An animal that feeds on its own kind.

carnivores Meat-eating animals.

cartilage A strong, stretchy type of body tissue, found in the skeleton.

cell The smallest basic unit of a plant or animal.

chordates A group of animals with a stiff rod running down their body.

civilization A human society with a highly developed social organization.

climate The usual weather conditions of a particular place.

continent A large land mass on the Earth's surface, surrounded mainly by ocean.

crust The Earth's outermost solid layer.

cuneiform An early type of writing done with a wedge-shaped stick.

descendant An animal or plant that has developed from its ancestor.

dinosaur A type of reptile with upright hind legs, a strong pelvis and a flexible neck.

domesticated A plant or animal that has been grown or bred by humans.

embryo An animal growing in its mother's womb or in an egg.

equator An imaginary line drawn around the middle of the Earth an equal distance from the North Pole and the South Pole.

evaporate To change from a liquid to a gas.

evolve To develop gradually.

extinct An animal that no longer exists. An animal becomes officially extinct if there have been no certain records of it for 50 years.

fleshy finned fish Fish with muscular fins that are edged with a fringe of fine rays.

fossil The remains of an animal or plant that has become embedded in rock.

habitat The natural surroundings in which an animal or plant lives.

herd Animals that live and feed as a group.

hominid A type of mammal that is able to walk upright, including modern humans.

horn Growth on an animal's head, made from the same substance that makes up fingernails and hair.

hunter-gatherers People who move from place to place, living on food they have caught or collected.

ice age A period when the temperature is very cold and masses of ice spread over large parts of the Earth.

invertebrates Animals that have no backbone.

lagoon A shallow body of water near a river or the sea.

living fossil A species of plant or animal that has remained relatively unchanged since prehistoric times.

mammals A group of warm-blooded vertebrates that have hair and feed their young with milk from their bodies.

marsupials A group of mammals with pouches, such as kangaroos and koalas.

menhir A large standing stone erected by people in prehistoric times.

migrate To travel to a different place in order to live there.

mineral A naturally occurring chemical found in crystal form in the ground.

monotremes A group of egg-laying mammals consisting only of the echidna and the platypus.

monument An old building or place which is built to honour a special event, or plays an important part in a country's history.

mya Million years ago.

photosynthesis The process by which a plant uses energy from the Sun to make food.

placentals Mammals that keep their babies inside their bodies until the babies are large enough to survive on their own.

plesiosaur A large type of extinct marine reptile that had a long neck and swam using four paddle-like flippers.

predator An animal that hunts, kills and eats other animals.

prehistory The story of life on Earth a very long time ago, before the earliest-known written records were made.

prey An animal that is hunted for food by other animals.

primate Mammals that have developed hands and feet, a short snout and a large brain.

pterosaur A type of extinct flying reptile that could produce its own heat.

ray finned fish Fish with delicate, fan-shaped fins, supported by fine, bony rods.

reptiles A group of animals that lay eggs on land and have scaly, waterproof skin.

species A group of animals or plants that have similar features and are able to join together to reproduce.

sponges The simplest multi-celled animals.

spore A reproductive cell made by some plants and simple organisms such as fungi.

Stone Age The earliest period in human prehistory, when tools and weapons were only made out of stone or bone.

tribe A group of people who live together and share the same language, culture and history.

tundra A large area of land where the ground is frozen in winter and it is too cold for trees to grow.

ultraviolet A type of light that is beyond violet in the spectrum.

vertebrates Animals with backbones.

volcano A mountain from with erupts lava, hot rocks and gasses.

warm-blooded Animals that can control their own body temperature so that it always stays the same, whatever the temperature of their surroundings.

Acknowledgements

Every effort has been made to trace the copyright holders of the material in this book. If any rights have been omitted, the publishers offer to rectify this in any subsequent editions following notification. The publishers are grateful to the following organizations and individuals for their permission to reproduce material (t=top, m=middle, b=bottom, l=left, r=right):

Corbis: **135bl** Bettmann/CORBIS; **143ml** Layne Kennedy/CORBIS; **151b** Nathan Benn/CORBIS; **171ml** Bettmann/CORBIS; **176br** Bettmann/CORBIS; **182m** Adam Woolfitt/CORBIS; **182bl** John Noble/CORBIS; **184tr** Bettmann/CORBIS
Digital Vision: **129 background**; **130-131 background**; **134bl**; **134-135 background**; **135 br**; **146-147 background**; **163m**; **123br**
Science Photo Library: **140l** Dr Kari Lounatmaa/Science Photo Library; **140r** Sinclair Stammers/Science Photo Library; **143tr** Sinclair Stammers/Science Photo Library; **143br** Victor Habbick Visions/Science Photo Library
Wildlight Photo Agency: **123ml**

Additional illustrators John Barber, Gary Bines, Giacinto Gaudenzi, Tony Gibson, Laura Hammonds, Bob Hersey, Phillip Hood, Inklink Firenze, Ian Jackson, Kevin Maddison, Peter Massey, Sean Milne, Luis Rey, Andrew Robinson, Luke Sargent, Chris Shields, Rod Sutterby, Franco Tempesta, David Wright

Additional designers Adam Constantine, Laura Hammonds and Joanne Kirkby

Quiz Answers
1C, 2B, 3C, 4D, 5C, 6A, 7A, 8D, 9C, 10B, 11B, 12A, 13D, 14B, 15D, 16A, 17C, 18C, 19D, 20A, 21D, 22D, 23C, 24C, 25C, 26B, 27A, 28B, 29B, 30A

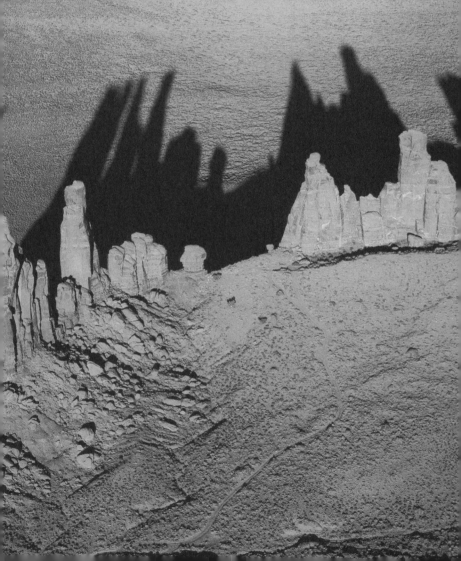

PLANET
EARTH

PLANET EARTH

Phillip Clarke

Designed by Karen Tomlins,
Michael Hill, Adam Constantine

Digital imagery by Keith Furnival

Consultant: Dr Roger Trend
Senior Lecturer in Earth Science
and Geography Education,
University of Exeter

Internet Links

Throughout this book, we have suggested interesting websites where you can find out more about Planet Earth. To visit the sites, go to the **Usborne Quicklinks website** at **www.usborne-quicklinks.com** and type the keywords "book of facts". There you will find links to click on to take you to all the sites. Here are some of the things you can do on the websites:

 Watch a volcano through a live webcam.

 Explore the wonders of Planet Earth in an interactive atlas.

 Try your hand at building an earthquake-proof skyscraper.

 See amazing photos of the Earth taken from space.

 See the North and South Poles through a live webcam.

Computer not essential

If you don't have access to the Internet, don't worry. This book is complete on its own.

Planet Earth Contents

Planet Earth

From out in space, the Earth looks like a small blue and green marble – yet it is home to over six billion people. There are trillions of stars in space, but we only know of a hundred or so planets, and Earth is the only one that we know for sure has life.

Right now, you are spinning at around 1,600kph. This is how quickly the Earth spins. It's also travelling around the Sun at 105,000kph. The Milky Way itself turns at 900,000kph. Feeling dizzy?

The Earth circles a star called the Sun. Scientists think that the Sun, Earth and our neighbouring planets were all made at the same time, about 4,600 million years ago.

The Sun is just one of over 200,000 million stars in our galaxy, the Milky Way. There are over 6,000 million galaxies in the universe.

YOU ARE HERE
The Sun is just one star in our huge galaxy...
Feeling small?

Round trip

It takes 28 days for the Moon to travel around the Earth. It takes a whole year for the Earth to travel around the Sun.

Earth

Moon

Sun

The Moon is about a quarter the size of the Earth.

Earth's statistics

Diameter	
at the Poles	12,714km
at the equator	12,756km
Circumference	
around Poles	39,942km
around equator	40,075km
Density	5.515g/cm³
Volume	1.1 million million km³
Total surface area	510 million km²
Mass	6,000 million million million tonnes

North and south

Four out of five people on Earth live in the northern half of the planet. More of the southern half is covered in sea.

The biggest ocean, the Pacific, is three times the size of the biggest continent, Asia.

Continent	Area (km²)
Asia	44,537,920
Africa	30,311,690
North America	22,656,190
South America	17,866,130
Antarctica	13,340,000
Europe	10,205,720
Oceania	8,564,400

The Pacific Ocean covers a third of the Earth.

INTERNET LINKS
To find links to websites about Planet Earth, go to **www.usborne-quicklinks.com**

Isolated isles

Bouvet Island in the Atlantic Ocean is the most isolated island on Earth. It is 1,600km from Africa and no one lives there. The most isolated lived-on island is Tristan da Cunha, 2,500km from Africa.

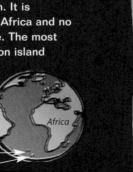

Africa

Tristan da Cunha
Bouvet Island

Largest islands	Area (km²)
Greenland	2,175,600
New Guinea	800,000
Borneo	751,100
Madagascar	587,040
Baffin Island, Canada	507,451
Sumatra, Indonesia	437,607
Honshu, Japan	230,455
Great Britain	229,870

At the Earth's Core

The Earth's rocky surface is called the crust. Under the oceans, the crust is 6km thick. Crust that makes up land is more like 40km thick. This may sound very thick, but if the Earth was an apple, its crust would only be as thick as the apple skin.

Earth's layers	Depth (km)	Temperature	Main content
Oceanic crust	6	500°C*	Basalt
Continental crust	40	500°C*	Granite
Mantle (radius)	2,870	1,500–3,000°C	Peridotite
Outer core (radius)	2,100	3,900°C	Liquid iron/nickel
Inner core (radius)	1,370	6,000°C	Solid iron/nickel

*This is the average temperature. It is 21°C near the surface.

The crust sits on a thicker layer of rock called the mantle. The rock here is hot enough to melt, but huge pressure squeezes it into a slow-moving solid.

Core blimey

The very middle of the Earth is called the core. It is thought to have an outer layer of liquid metal with a solid inner core – but of course no one's been there to check.

! Scientists believe that the Earth's solid core is a huge iron crystal. Digging down to it would take a while though, as it lies more than 4,800km below the Earth's surface.

Layer upon layer

Geologists – scientists who study the Earth's structure – divide its crust and mantle into more layers:

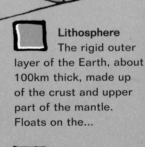

Lithosphere The rigid outer layer of the Earth, about 100km thick, made up of the crust and upper part of the mantle. Floats on the...

Asthenosphere A hot, semi-liquid layer of the mantle, which is about 200km thick.

Crust

Inner core

Mantle

Outer core

How do they know?

Geologists have lots of ways of finding out about the Earth's insides:

Drilling

The Kola Superdeep Borehole in Russia is the world's deepest borehole, at 12.3km; yet it still only scratches the Earth's surface.

The deeper you drill into the crust, the older are the rocks. At the bottom of the Kola hole, rock dates back 2,800 million years – not long after the first plants appeared on Earth.

Earthquakes

Studying the paths of shockwaves caused by earthquakes has led geologists to believe that the Earth's outer core is liquid, while its mantle and inner core are solid.

Meteorites

Asteroids are rocks out in space. They are thought to be left over from when the planets formed and to be made of the same stuff. Meteorites are pieces of asteroid that fall to Earth. Studying these helps geologists work out what types of rock are hidden deep inside our own planet.

Monster magnet

Our planet is a huge magnet. Its magnetism is thought to be caused by its liquid outer core swirling around the inner core. If you've used a compass, you'll have seen Earth's magnetism at work. Compasses, though, don't point to the true North Pole, as the Earth's magnetic poles wander slowly over thousands of years. Navigators need to know how far apart the true and magnetic poles are to use maps accurately.

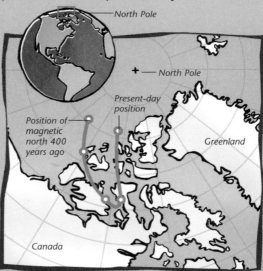

North Pole

North Pole

Present-day position

Position of magnetic north 400 years ago

Greenland

Canada

The Earth's magnetic poles slowly wander around the globe, even switching places completely every 250,000 years or so.

INTERNET LINKS
To find links to websites about the inside of the Earth, go to **www.usborne-quicklinks.com**

Scientists used to think the Earth was hollow and could be entered through holes at the Poles. In 1838, a group went to find the way in at the South Pole. They didn't find a hole, but did find land. This proved that Antarctica was more than just a frozen sea.

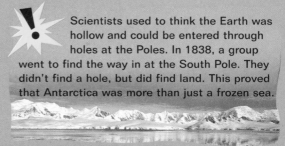

The Changing Earth

Scientists think that the Earth was made 4,600 million years ago from a spinning cloud of dust and gas. The cloud shrank into hot, molten balls.

Earth started life as a great ball of fire.

As the balls cooled, some of them hardened and gravity pulled them together to form rocky planets: Mercury, Venus, Mars and Earth.

! The Moon was probably formed 4,500 million years ago, after a cosmic collision between the Earth and another planet the size of Mars. Rocky rubble from the crash exploded outwards and gradually formed the Moon you see today.

Giant jigsaw

Earth's outer shell isn't a single piece. It is broken into smaller pieces called tectonic plates. These drift on top of a semi-liquid layer in the Earth's mantle*. Oceanic (undersea) plates are much thinner than continental (land-bearing) plates.

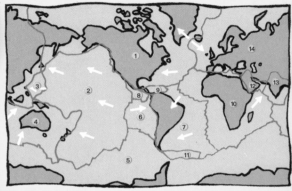

The Earth's plates → *Direction of drift*

1. North American
2. Pacific
3. Philippine
4. Australian
5. Antarctic
6. Nazca
7. South American
8. Cocos
9. Caribbean
10. African
11. Scotia
12. Arabian
13. Indian
14. Eurasian

Crumpled crust

As plates drift, they collide and crumple. Continental plates that meet buckle upwards to form mountain ranges. Tibet, for example, has risen over 3km in the last two million years. Oceanic plates plunge beneath continental plates, forming deep ocean trenches.

The Moon may once have been part of the Earth.

Slip sliding away

When plates slide past each other, they form big cracks, called faults. The San Andreas Fault, in the USA, stretches for over 1,000km through California to Mexico. Over 15 million years, western California has moved 300km north-west

Part of the San Andreas Fault

*See page 200

Mountain high

The longest mountain range, the Mid-Atlantic Ridge, is under the sea. It is 11,000km long. It forms where liquid rock wells up between plates, cooling to form new rock.

Iceland

Iceland is part of the Mid-Atlantic Ridge that rises above sea level.

Millions of years ago, North Africa was covered in ice and Antarctica was covered in rainforest. The Earth's plates drift, so even continents don't always stay in the same place.

Once upon a time in Antarctica...

INTERNET LINKS
To find links to websites about the Earth's formation, and its plates, go to **www.usborne-quicklinks.com**

When plates collide

The boundaries between plates have names describing how the plates affect each other and what happens to the landscape when they meet.

Plate boundary		Landscape
Constructive: *Plates pull apart; magma (liquid rock) wells up and cools to form new crust.*		Spreading ridge, for example, the Mid-Atlantic Ridge
Destructive: *One plate dives under another, and melts back into mantle.*		Ocean trench, for example, the Mariana Trench (see *Undersea landscape*, page 235)
Conservative: *Plates rub past each other, causing earthquakes.*		Transform fault, for example, the San Andreas Fault

Continental drift

Earth's plates drift no faster than your nails grow. But over millions of years, this slow movement can dramatically change the layout of the continents and oceans.

200 million years ago

200 million years ago, most of the Earth's land was joined in one huge continent, called Pangaea.

50 million years ago

50 million years ago, the land began to form the continents we know today.

50 million years from now?

As the plates continue to drift, Earth may one day look like this.

Earth's Atmosphere

The Earth is wrapped in a blanket of air called the atmosphere. The atmosphere is made up of several different layers. The highest layer stretches up into space, 8,000km above Earth.

Flying high

All the weather happens in the troposphere – the layer of atmosphere that hugs the Earth's surface. This is the only layer that contains enough water vapour to make clouds.

Big thunder clouds have flat tops where they hit the next layer of the atmosphere.

If all the water in the atmosphere fell in one massive downpour, it would cover the Earth's surface with 2.5cm of water.

2.5cm —

Layer	Height	Temperature
Exosphere	500–8,000km	2,200°C+
Thermosphere	80–500km	-80°C to 2,200°C
Mesosphere	50–80km	10°C to -80°C
Stratosphere	8–50km	-55°C to 10°C
Troposphere		

Troposphere
Height over equator   16km   At 16km   -55°C
Height over Poles   8km   At sea level 15°C

Gasping for air

The higher you go, the less air there is and the dizzier you get. This is why some mountaineers carry extra oxygen to breathe. The amount of oxygen at the top of Everest is just a third of the amount at sea level.

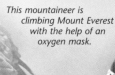

This mountaineer is climbing Mount Everest with the help of an oxygen mask.

Gases in the air

Nitrogen	78.0%
Oxygen	21.0%
Argon	0.9%
Carbon dioxide	0.03%
Other gases	0.07%

e.g. neon, helium, krypton, hydrogen, xenon, ozone

Breathe easy

The oxygen on Earth is 3,000 million years old. It began forming when simple, plant-like cells, called blue-green bacteria, appeared on the Earth. Plants in sunlight make oxygen, which all animals, including us, need to breathe.

Blue-green bacteria – tiny oxygen factories

Height records

Vehicle	Height
Space Shuttle	623.6km
Unmanned balloon	53.0km
Mig-25 fighter plane	38.0km
Manned balloon	35.0km
Concorde	19.0km
Boeing-747 Jumbo jet	13.0km
DC-10 plane	12.2km

For comparison, Mount Everest is 8.9km high

Radio waves

Radio waves move at the speed of light (300,000km per second). The signals travel around the curve of the Earth by bouncing off tiny particles in the atmosphere.

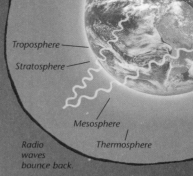

Troposphere

Stratosphere

Mesosphere

Thermosphere

Radio waves bounce back.

INTERNET LINKS
To find links to websites about the Earth's atmosphere, go to **www.usborne-quicklinks.com**

Sun screen

The Sun isn't just a life-giver. It has damaging rays as well. High up in the stratosphere is a layer of ozone gas. Luckily for us, this filters out most of them.

Without the ozone layer to protect us from harmful ultraviolet rays, there would be no life on Earth.

A big volcanic eruption can throw dust and ash up into the stratosphere. This can travel halfway across the world and take up to three years to fall back to Earth.

Mount St Helens spouting ash

Ozone layer

Rocks

Rocks are pieces of the Earth's crust. There are three main types:

Igneous rocks form when liquid rock, called magma, rises from the mantle, cools and becomes solid.

Sedimentary rocks are made from mud, sand or other stuff, called sediment, that has been squashed down into layers over millions of years. You can find fossils in this type of rock.

Metamorphic rocks are made from other rocks that have been changed by the massive pressure and heat inside the Earth. *Metamorphic* is from the Greek words for "changed shape".

Granite *A hard, coarse-grained rock formed beneath the crust. Coloured pink to grey. It makes up most of the continental crust.*

Chalk *A soft rock, usually white; contains shells, and plant and animal remains.*

Slate *Formed from shale (a fine-grained sedimentary rock) under high pressure. Splits easily into thin sheets.*

Basalt *A hard, fine-grained rock formed in lava* flows. It is younger than granite and makes up most of the oceanic crust.*

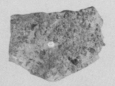

Limestone *A hard rock; often contains many shells; usually white to grey, but may be red or honey-coloured.*

Marble *Formed from limestone warped by heat*

Obsidian *A black or greenish natural glass made when lava cools very quickly above ground in a volcanic eruption.*

Sandstone *A rock formed from the sands of beaches, rivers or deserts.*

Quartzite *Formed from sandstone changed by high pressure and heat*

Stones can float – at least, a pumice stone can. This is because it's full of trapped gas bubbles. It is an igneous rock made when lava cools quickly in a volcanic explosion.

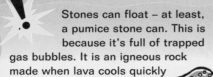

INTERNET LINKS
To find out how to start your own rock collection, identify rocks, watch a cartoon history of the Earth, play some rocking online games and more besides, go to **www.usborne-quicklinks.com**

*Lava is magma flowing above the ground or seabed.

Rock recycling

Over millions of years, natural forces above and inside the Earth change rocks from one type into another.

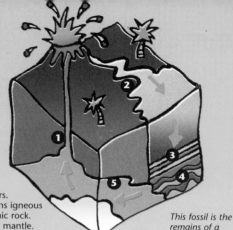

Key

1 Igneous rock is formed as magma, rising from the mantle, cools.
2 Wind, rain and rivers wear away bare igneous rock. Pieces of sediment are carried to the sea.
3 Sediment settles on the seafloor. Over many years, it is packed into rock layers.
4 Heat and pressure under the Earth turns igneous and sedimentary rock into metamorphic rock.
5 Metamorphic rock melts back into the mantle.

This fossil is the remains of a prehistoric shellfish.

Rock	Uses
Clay	Bricks. Paper making
Coal	Fuel
Feldspar	Porcelain making
Granite	Building
Limestone	Building. Steelmaking
Marble	Decorative stonework
Sandstone	Building

Fossils

The remains or shapes of living things that died long ago can be found in sedimentary rock. The original remains have usually rotted away, but they may be replaced with sediment or minerals which hold the shape together.

This rock formation in Arizona, USA, is made from prehistoric sand dunes that were slowly squeezed together.

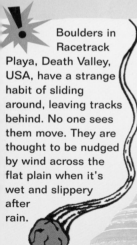

Boulders in Racetrack Playa, Death Valley, USA, have a strange habit of sliding around, leaving tracks behind. No one sees them move. They are thought to be nudged by wind across the flat plain when it's wet and slippery after rain.

Minerals

Minerals are made in the Earth. Rocks are made up of different types of minerals. The chart below shows the main types of minerals that can be found in the Earth's crust.

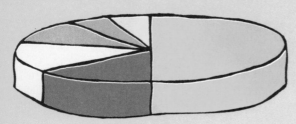

	Feldspar 50%		Quartz 15%		Olivine 5%
	Pyroxenes and amphiboles 15%		Micas and clays 10%		Other 5%

Rock recipe

This close-up view of granite shows the minerals that make it up.

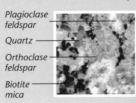

Plagioclase feldspar

Quartz

Orthoclase feldspar

Biotite mica

Mineral ID

Scientists identify minerals by the following:

Colour
Impurities in minerals make colours vary.

Traces of iron turn clear quartz into purple amethyst.

Streak
A mineral's colour may vary, but the streak it makes usually stays the same.

Haematite makes a red streak.

Lustre
The way a mineral shines

Citrine has a glassy lustre.

Cleavage
The way a mineral breaks

Some minerals break into sheets...   *...others break into blocks.*

Hardness
(See the Mohs scale opposite.)

Common minerals	Mineral group	Colour	Found in
Plagioclase	Feldspars	White–grey	Gabbro
Orthoclase	Feldspars	White–pink	Granite
Quartz	Quartz	Clear–various	Many rocks
Haematite	Oxides	Red–brown–black	Sandstone
Halite	Halides	Clear–white	Carbonates
Calcite	Carbonates	Clear–white	Limestone
Gypsum	Sulphates	White	Carbonates
Olivine	Olivines	Olive green	Basalt
Garnet	Garnets	Any but blue	Schist; gneiss
Augite	Pyroxenes	Brown–green–black	Gabbro
Hornblende	Amphiboles	Black–dark green	Igneous rocks
Biotite	Micas	Brown–black	Many rocks
Muscovite	Micas	White	Many rocks
Kaolinite	Clays	White–pink–grey	Mudstones
Copper	Elements	Copper	Porphyry

Mohs hardness scale

A mineral can scratch those rated below it in this scale.

Hardness	Scratched by
1 Talc	Fingernail, easily
2 Gypsum	Fingernail
3 Calcite	Knife, very easily
4 Fluorite	Knife, easily
5 Apatite	Knife, just
	Scratches
6 Orthoclase	Glass, just
7 Quartz	Glass, easily
8 Topaz	Glass, very easily
9 Corundum	Cuts glass
10 Diamond	Corundum

Seeing double

If you look through a crystal of Iceland Spar, you will see a double image. Iceland Spar is a type of calcite. As rays of light pass through it, it splits them in two.

You'll look twice at Iceland Spar.

Glow stones

Some minerals can give off light. Fluorite glows blue if it's placed under ultraviolet light. This effect is called "fluorescence", after the mineral.

Quartz glowing red and fluorite glowing blue in ultraviolet light.

Cool crystals

When magma cools it usually forms into regular, geometric solids called crystals. A crystal's shape depends on the way the atoms and molecules join inside it.

Cubic crystal

Triclinic crystal

Orthorhombic crystal

Tetragonal crystal

Monoclinic crystal

Hexagonal crystal

Lightning can make shapes in sand. When it strikes sand, pieces of natural glass, called fulgurites, may be formed. The intense heat vaporizes and melts the sand, fusing it into hollow, branch-like shapes which follow the path taken by the lightning.

A solid lightning bolt?

INTERNET LINKS
To find links to marvellous websites about minerals, go to **www.usborne-quicklinks.com**

Precious Stones

Gemstones are celebrities of the mineral world because they are so rare and beautiful. Of the hundred or so types that exist, diamonds, emeralds, rubies and sapphires are the most precious.

The Star of Africa

This is the world's largest transparent cut diamond. There are larger coloured diamonds, but clear ones are worth more. This pear-shaped jewel was cut from the largest clear diamond ever found: the 3,106 carat* South African Cullinan diamond.

The Star of Africa is in the British royal sceptre. In real life, it's twice as big as this.

Gemstone cuts

Like getting a haircut in a style that suits you, gemstones are cut in a way to enhance their beauty.

Cut		Information
Cabochon cut		A smooth, dome shape. Used for dark stones and gems made from living things, such as amber.
Round brilliant cut		Increases a gem's ability to catch the light. Used very widely for diamonds.
Emerald step cut		Increases the intensity of a gem's colour. Used for coloured stones.
Cushion mixed cut		Used for transparent coloured gems, such as rubies and sapphires.
Marquise fancy cut		Makes a small gem appear larger

The Hope Diamond

Legend has it that this large, deep blue diamond was stolen from an Indian temple hundreds of years ago and brings bad luck. It once belonged to Louis XIV of France and, later, to the English Hope family.

Louis XIV

Diamond, the hardest mineral, is made of carbon, the same element that makes up graphite – the crumbly, black stuff in pencil leads. Diamonds form much deeper in the Earth than graphite, so the greater pressure squeezes them into a stronger structure.

Diamond and pencil lead... the same basic stuff

The Star of India

One of the largest sapphires is called the Star of India. It is deep blue with a star pattern inside and was found hundreds of years ago in Sri Lanka.

*When measuring diamonds, 5 carats = 1 gram.

Diamond geysers

Diamonds form deep down. They are only found near the surface if they were forced up millions of years ago with magma from the mantle, through a rare and violent type of volcano. The cooling magma formed pipe-shaped masses of rock.

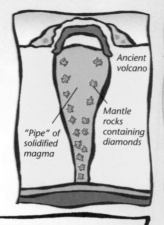

Ancient volcano

Mantle rocks containing diamonds

"Pipe" of solidified magma

Jade – a precious green or white stone – is as tough as steel. It was highly prized in ancient China, and was used to make axes, knives and other weapons.

Not just a pretty sword – jade blades were strong and sharp.

INTERNET LINKS
To find links to websites about jewels and gemstones, go to **www.usborne-quicklinks.com**

Birthstones

Month	Gemstone	Colour	Symbolizes	Mineral	Best gems found
January	Garnet		Loyalty	Hard silicate	Brazil; Russia
February	Amethyst		Sincerity	Quartz	Zambia; Uruguay
March	Aquamarine		Courage	Beryl	Brazil
April	Diamond		Innocence	Pure carbon	South Africa
May	Emerald		Love	Beryl	Colombia
June	Pearl		Health	Calcium carbonate	Persian Gulf
July	Ruby		Contentment	Corundum	Burma
August	Peridot		Happy marriage	Olivine	Arizona; Pakistan
September	Sapphire		Clear thinking	Corundum	Sri Lanka; Burma
October	Opal		Hope	Silica with water	Australia
November	Topaz		Faithfulness	Silicate	Brazil
December	Turquoise		Prosperity	Copper silicate	Iran

Earthquakes

There are about a million earthquakes a year. They are caused by the shifting of the Earth's plates. Most are so tiny that they only show up on special measuring devices, called seismographs. Big quakes occur about every two weeks, but most of these happen under the sea.

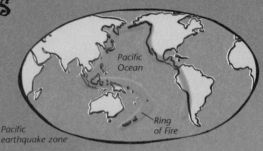

Pacific Ocean

Ring of Fire

Pacific earthquake zone

Ring of Fire

The most earthquake-prone place in the world is an area circling the Pacific Ocean, called the Ring of Fire. Nine out of ten quakes happen there.

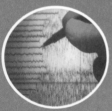

A seismograph records earthquake vibrations as lines on paper.

INTERNET LINKS
To find links to ground-breaking websites about earthquakes, go to **www.usborne-quicklinks.com**

Some animals act strangely when they sense an earthquake coming. In 1975, the people of Haicheng, China, noticed snakes waking early from hibernation. Thousands fled, escaping a huge earthquake, partly thanks to these animal warnings.

Rating rumbles

The power of an earthquake is measured on the Richter scale. Each whole value has 33 times the energy of the one below. Earthquake intensity is measured on the Mercalli scale, which rates effects.

Mercalli	Richter	Effects
1	0.1-2.9	Detectable only by seismometers
2	3.0-3.4	Noticed by a few people on upper floors
3	3.5-4.0	Like a light truck going by. Hanging lights swing.
4	4.1-4.4	Like a heavy truck going by. Windows rattle.
5	4.5-4.8	Sleepers wake up. Small items move. Drinks spill.
6	4.9-5.4	Many people run outside. Heavy furniture moves.
7	5.5-6.0	Walls crack. Loose bricks fall. Hard to stand up.
8	6.1-6.5	Chimneys and weak buildings collapse.
9	6.6-7.0	Well-built houses collapse. Ground cracks.
10	7.1-7.3	Landslides. Many stone buildings collapse.
11	7.4-8.1	Most buildings destroyed. Large cracks in ground.
12	8.2+	Ground moves in waves. Total destruction.

Ten minute terror

Earthquakes usually last less than a minute. The terrible earthquake that destroyed Lisbon, Portugal, in 1755 lasted for a whole ten minutes.

The shockwaves of the 1755 Lisbon earthquake were felt as far as North Africa and Scotland.

 *See Giant jigsaw, page 202

Recent major earthquakes	Richter	Deaths	Notes
2003, Boumerdes, Algeria	6.9	2,200	Widespread damage; tsunami waves
2001, Gujarat, India	8.0	20,085	Second strongest quake in Indian history
1995, Kobe, Japan	6.8	6,400	Thousands of buildings destroyed
1990, Manjil-Rudbar, Iran	7.7	50,000	Landslides; cities destroyed
1985, Mexico City, Mexico	8.1	20,000	Thousands of buildings destroyed
1976, Tangshan, China	7.9	655,237	Deadliest 20th century quake
1970, Coast of Peru	7.8	18,000	Town of Yungay buried in rockslide
1964, Prince William Sound, Alaska	8.6	125	Strongest quake in USA's history
1960, Concepcion, Chile	8.7	2,000	Strongest quake ever recorded
1935, Quetta, Pakistan	7.5	30-60,000	Most of city of Quetta destroyed
1923, Tokyo-Kanto, Japan	8.3	142,807	Caused the Great Tokyo Fire
1920, Ningxia-Kansu, China	8.6	200,000	Huge cracks in ground; landslides
1908, Messina, Italy	7.5	70-100,000	Tsunami killed many
1906, San Francisco	7.9	3,000	Deadliest in USA's history; Great Fire

China crisis

China has the worst record for earthquake deaths. In 1556, an earthquake in Shanxi province killed 830,000 people – the deadliest earthquake ever.

In the worst earthquakes, the ground rolls in huge waves of destruction. The 1964 Alaskan earthquake lasted seven minutes and cracks opened in the ground up to 90cm wide and 12m deep. One school was split in two.

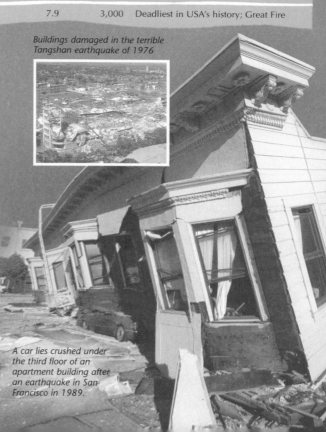

Buildings damaged in the terrible Tangshan earthquake of 1976

A car lies crushed under the third floor of an apartment building after an earthquake in San Francisco in 1989.

Volcanoes

There are over 600 active volcanoes on Earth. About half of these are on the Ring of Fire*. Many islands, such as Iceland, are volcanic. Iceland has about 200 volcanoes.

Living dangerously

Ash from volcanoes can make the soil rich. But ash and lava from big eruptions can ruin land for years. Farmers have to hope for the best.

Living by a volcano can be risky.

Eruptions

About 20–30 volcanoes erupt each year. A few erupt almost all the time – Stromboli in Italy goes off every 20 minutes.

Stromboli – little and often

Some volcanoes are dormant (asleep), and can go for years without erupting. In 1902, Mount Pelée, on the island of Martinique, erupted after 50 years of being dormant, killing 29,000 people.

Beware of sleeping volcanoes.

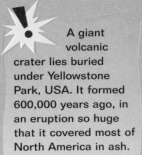

A giant volcanic crater lies buried under Yellowstone Park, USA. It formed 600,000 years ago, in an eruption so huge that it covered most of North America in ash.

Castle Geyser in Yellowstone Park, USA, is powered by a giant underground volcano.

Volcano	Location	Last major eruption	Largest eruption	Facts
Kilauea	Hawaii, USA	continual	1983–now	Most active volcano on Earth
Mt Erebus	Ross Island, Antarctica	continual	1841	Southernmost active volcano
Mt Etna	Sicily, Italy	1992	1669	Europe's highest (3,236m) and liveliest
Nevado del Ruiz	Colombia	1985	1595	Deadliest recent eruption: 24,000 killed
Mauna Loa	Hawaii, USA	1984	1950	Largest active volcano (5,271km^2)
Mt St Helens	Washington, USA	1980	2000BC	Largest eruption in US history (1980)
Vesuvius	Naples, Italy	1944	AD79	Eruption in AD79 destroyed Pompeii
Ojos del Salado	Chile/Argentina	unknown	unknown	Highest active volcano (6,887m)
Krakatau	Sumatra, Indonesia	1883	1883	Made loudest sound ever recorded
Mt Tambora	Sumbawa, Indonesia	1815	1815	Largest eruption in history
Mt Fuji	Honshu, Japan	1708	930BC	Highest mountain (3,776m) in Japan

Baby boomer

In a Mexican cornfield in 1943, the volcano Paricutín was born. It began as a 45m crack, spitting ash and scaring farmhands.

A crack in the Earth became a volcano.

Within a few months, its lava flows were 15m deep. In a year, it had a cone higher than the Eiffel Tower in France. In 1952, after nine years of destroying villages and crops, Paricutín's life came to an end.

Mount Etna in Sicily has the strange habit of blowing rings of steam. They measure 200m across, last up to ten minutes, and may rise 1km into the air.

I'm forever blowing steam rings...

Rivers of fire

Lava is hot magma (molten rock) flowing above the Earth's surface. There are two types of lava flow. They have Hawaiian names, because much volcano study is done in Hawaii.

aa (say "ah-ah")
Stodgy, slow-flowing lava with a rough, broken surface. Forms cone-shaped "stratovolcanoes" from violent eruptions.

pahoehoe (say "pa-hoy-hoy")
Runny, fizzy lava with a thin skin, often with rope-like wrinkles. Forms dome volcanoes from gentle eruptions.

As lava from Kilauea, in Hawaii, flows into the Pacific Ocean, it cools to form new land.

INTERNET LINKS
To see a volcano through a live webcam, and much more, go to
www.usborne-quicklinks.com

Mountains

Around a quarter of Earth's land is covered with mountains that rise 900m or more above sea level. Tibet, in China, is the highest country, averaging 4,572m.

Mountain roots

Just as ships float in water, so also Earth's rocky plates "float" on the denser layer below. As mountains grow, their weight presses the crust down into the mantle, forming roots that act like foundations.

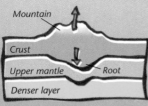

Mountains have roots that push down into the Earth's mantle.

Mountain pile-up

Where continental plates smash together, mountains are built. Ten million years ago, India crashed into Asia. The Asian plate slowly buckled upwards, forming the Himalayas – the highest mountains in the world.

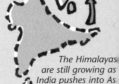

The Himalayas are still growing as India pushes into As

Mountain ranges	Location	Million years old
Highlands	Scotland	400
Appalachians	USA	250
Urals	Russia	250
Andes	South America	80
Rockies	North America	70
Himalayas	Asia	40
Alps	Europe	15

Old as the hills

All mountain ranges are millions of years old but the tallest ranges, such as the Himalayas, are often younger than the shorter ones. They haven't had so much time to get worn down.

The Himalayas are new kids on the block.

Huge footprints have been found in the Himalayas that don't match any known animal. Many people believe that they are made by giant, ape-like creatures called yetis.

Were these footprints made by man or beast?

Continent	Highest mountain	Height	Location
Asia	Mount Everest	8,850m	Nepal/China
South America	Mount Aconcagua	6,959m	Argentina
North America	Mount McKinley	6,194m	USA
Africa	Mount Kilimanjaro	5,895m	Tanzania
Europe	Mount Elbrus	5,642m	Russia
Antarctica	Vinson Massif	4,897m	Ellsworth Land
Oceania	Mount Wilhelm	4,509m	Papua New Guinea

INTERNET LINKS
To find links to websites about mountains, go to **www.usborne-quicklinks.com**

City high

The world's highest capital city is La Paz in Bolivia. It is 3,632m up in the Andes. That's more than a third as high as Mount Everest.

La Paz in Bolivia is known as "the city that touches the sky".

Rocky Mountain goats can climb cliffs that are nearly vertical. Their sharp hoofs dig into rock and ice, and have tough pads underneath that act as suction cups, stopping them from slipping.

Each half of the hoof can move separately for better grip.

Big hearted

Some people live very high up, where there is less oxygen in the air. The Quechua Indians live 4,000m up in the Andes. Mountain people and animals have big hearts and lungs to carry more blood, and so more oxygen.

High life

Different plants and animals are found at different heights up a mountain. Here are some of the highlights of Himalayan life:

8,000m

Alpine chough

Cushion pinks

Snow leopard

5,000m

Tibetans take their yaks as high as 4,600m to graze in the summer.

Blue poppy

3,000m

Red panda

Tibetans have terraced the lower slopes to grow their crops.

1,000m

Longest mountain ranges	Location	Length
Andes	South America	7,240km
Rocky Mountains	North America	6,030km
Himalaya/Karakoram/Hindu Kush	Asia	3,860km
Great Dividing Range	Australia	3,620km
Transantarctic Mountains	Antarctica	3,540km

Caves and Caverns

Caves prove that water can be stronger than rock. Water flowing underground slowly eats away at rocks until they collapse, forming caves and caverns (which are just large caves).

Cave critters

Cave animals are adapted to their cold, dark homes. Because it is so dark, some are blind and use other senses to find their way around. Many don't have skin colour to protect them from the Sun's rays.

Name	Adaptations to cave life
Little brown bat	Find their way by bouncing echoes off objects ("echo location")
Olm (cave salamander)	Blind; pale skin; sharp sense of smell; can go without food for long periods
Northern cavefish	Blind; pale skin; vibration sensors on head; carry young in gills
Cave cricket	Very long legs to clamber over rocks; colour camouflages against limestone

In Mexico, there are some deep caves with walls that drip burning acid. In spite of this, tiny, living things called bacteria live here. They mix with minerals to form dangling strands of acid slime known as "snottites".

These slimy formations are called snottites – remind you of anything?

To the Batcave!

Bracken Cave in Texas, USA, houses the world's largest bat colony. Up to 20 million Mexican free-tailed bats call it home.

The bats of Bracken Cave can eat 250 tonnes of insects in a night.

Water sculptures

Water that drips through and over cavern rock contains dissolved minerals. These minerals can slowly build up into strange and beautiful shapes. Cavers have given names to some of these shapes:

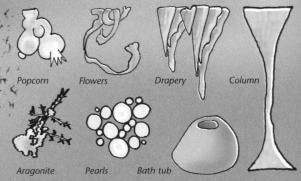

Popcorn   *Flowers*   *Drapery*   *Column*

Aragonite   *Pearls*   *Bath tub*

Underground wonders	Country	Record
Mammoth Cave	USA	Longest cave system (563km)
Gouffre Mirolda/ Lucien Bouclier	France	Deepest cave (1.73km)
Sarawak Chamber	Malaysia	Largest cavern (700m long; 300m wide; 70m high)
Sistema Chac-Mol	Mexico	Longest stalactite (12m)
Cueva San Martin Infierno	Cuba	Tallest stalagmite (67.2m)
Tham Sao Hin	Thailand	Tallest column (61.5m)
Ruby Falls	USA	Highest undergound waterfall (44m)
Son Trach river	Vietnam	Longest underground river (11.3km)
Kazumura Cave	USA	Longest lava tube (65.5km)
Painted Cave	USA	Longest sea cave (374m)

Stalactites grow down from the roof.

Stalagmites grow up from the floor.

Cave art

In 1940, two adventurous boys discovered some caves in Lascaux, France. On the cave walls, they were amazed to find beautiful paintings of horses, bison and other animals, painted 17,000 years ago.

Stone-age graffiti?

INTERNET LINKS
To find links to amazing websites about caves and caverns, go to
www.usborne-quicklinks.com

The world's tallest underground room is in Baiyu Dong cave, China. It is 424m high.

Can you imagine a room as tall as New York's Empire State Building?

Crystal caverns

Deep in the Naica mines in Mexico are the world's largest known crystals. These are giant gypsum crystals that have formed in the hot, sauna-like atmosphere of a single cavern. Some, measuring 15m high, are as tall as pine trees.

The Cave of the Giants lives up to its name.

Tundra

About a tenth of Earth's land is covered by a huge, frozen area called the tundra. It stretches between the Arctic ice and the Northern forests.

Tundra

Permanent frost

The frozen layer of soil beneath the tundra never thaws, and is called the permafrost. In parts of Siberia it can be as deep as 1.5km.

Tundra

Permafrost

The permafrost stops water draining away, so in summer the tundra is riddled with bogs and ponds.

Deep freeze

The permafrost can act like a deep freeze. Well-preserved remains of Ice Age mammoths have been found in Siberia and Alaska – even whole bodies.

Over 50 deep-frozen mammoths have been found in the permafrost.

Shaggy goat story

Musk oxen may look like bison but they are actually related to goats and are very nimble for their size. They live all year in the tundra. Their shaggy hair grows down nearly to their hoofs, keeping them warm.

Only humans can grow longer hair than musk oxen.

Tundra people

People have lived in the tundra for thousands of years. Here are some native tundra people.

People	Where they live	Population
Sakha	Russia	400,000
Komi	Russia	344,500
Inuit	Russia, Alaska, Greenland, Canada	130,000
Sami	Russia, Sweden, Finland, Norway	100,000
Eskimo	Alaska, Russia	48,500
Indian tribes	Alaska	36,500
Nenet	Russia	34,500
Even	Russia	17,000
Chukchi	Russia	15,000

Tundra statistics

Area	13,000,000km²
Permafrost depth (average)	305-610m
Winter temperature	-29 to -33°C
Summer temperature	3 to 12°C

Winter white

As winter approaches, many tundra animals turn white to blend in with the snow. In spring, they change back. Here are some animals in their winter colours.

Ptarmigan

Snowshoe rabbit

Snowy owl

Stoat

Arctic fox

In winter, the north-east Siberian tundra under its layer of snow and ice becomes even colder than the North Pole.

Oil highway

The Trans-Alaskan oil pipeline stretches 1,300km from the Arctic Ocean to southern Alaska. It has to be heated to at least 45°C to stop the oil freezing inside the pipe.

The pipeline is raised in places to let large animals get under.

Watch your step in the tundra – you could be walking on top of a forest. Near the treeline, the trees are so blasted by the wind that they cling to the ground.

Ground willow can be 5m long but only 10cm high.

Red hot

Many tundra plants have striking, dark red leaves. This helps them to soak up as much of the Sun's life-giving heat as they can in the cold climate.

Red bearberry leaves

INTERNET LINKS
To find links to websites about the tundra, go to www.usborne-quicklinks.com

Commuter caribou

Huge herds of up to 100,000 caribou (North American reindeer) trek 600km north to the tundra each spring to give birth. They return south every autumn. Caribou have been following the same routes for hundreds of years.

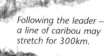

Following the leader – a line of caribou may stretch for 300km.

Northern Forests

The largest forest area in the world is called the taiga (say "tie-ga"). It stretches from Alaska to Canada, and from Scandinavia to Siberia.

■ Taiga
■ Deciduous forest

Most of the trees in the taiga are conifers. These have needles rather than broad leaves, and are mostly evergreen. Their seeds are protected in woody cones.

Further south (see map), the forests are broad-leaved and deciduous. This means that the trees lose their leaves in autumn.

Conifers

Red cedar

Cypress

Hemlock

Larch

Spruce

Juniper

Silver fir

Douglas fir

Yew

Pine

Redwood

Part of conifer	Used for
Timber	Furniture, matches, tannic acid (used in making leather goods)
Pulp	Paper, plastics, Rayon
Cellulose	Cellophane, turpentine
Needles	Pine oil (used in soap), vitamins A and E

King cone

The longest pine cones come from sugar pines in the USA. They grow 66cm long – nearly two-thirds the length of a baseball bat.

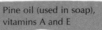

Sugar pine cone

Nearly three-quarters of the world's timber and almost all of the world's paper comes from conifers. Paper is made from leftover timber cuttings and thin trees. From one tree, you could make 800 copies of this book.

INTERNET LINKS
To find links to tremendous websites about trees, go to **www.usborne-quicklinks.com**

All change

The most amazing thing about deciduous trees is the way their leaves change colour before they fall in autumn. This is because their leaves lose a green chemical called chlorophyll as they die. With the green colour gone, other colours in the leaf are revealed.

Autumn leaves go out in a blaze of colour.

Each person in the USA uses enough wooden items a year to make a tree 30m tall and 41cm wide. That's over 280 million trees a year. Using recycled paper saves trees.

Many recycled products show this symbol.

Broad-leaved deciduous trees

Ash

Alder

Oak

Birch

Beech

Maple

Elm

Chestnut

Record-breaking trees

Giant sequoia, California, USA	Largest tree ("General Sherman") 31m around trunk; 83.8m tall
Montezuma cypress, Oaxaca, Mexico	Broadest tree ("El Tule") 36m around trunk
Aspen grove, Utah, USA	A grove of quaking aspen ("Pando"), which is joined at the roots, making it the largest living thing, at 0.81km² in area.
Coast redwood, California, USA	Tallest tree (the "Mendocino tree") 112m
Bristlecone pine, California, USA	Oldest tree ("Methuselah") 4,767 years

Fireproof trees

Trees with thick bark, such as pine and sequoia, can survive fierce forest fires. These tough trees are only scarred by the fire and their wood is unharmed. Some forest fires spread at 15kph and the roar they make can be heard 1.6km away.

Coast redwoods, a type of sequoia, are the tallest trees in the world. They can grow over five times the height of a house.

Tropical Rainforests

Rainforests stretch around the middle of the Earth like a green belt. These ancient forests have broad-leaved evergreen trees that are home to Earth's most amazing variety of animals.

Tropical rainforests are hot and wet. At least 250cm of rain falls there each year.

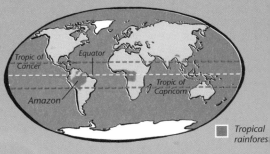

Tropic of Cancer
Equator
Tropic of Capricorn
Amazon

Tropical rainforest

INTERNET LINKS
To find links to websites about the world's rainforests, go to **www.usborne-quicklinks.com**

Jeepers creepers

Lianas are giant, woody vines that climb trees and hang down from the rainforest canopy. The longest are over 1km.

Lianas are strong enough for monkeys (and Tarzan) to swing on

Rainforest layers

Emergent layer
Huge trees mushroom through the layer below, searching for sunlight. Some are as tall as a twelve-floor building.

Canopy
Broad treetops make a forest roof, tied together with vines. The canopy is so thick, rain can take ten minutes to reach the forest floor. Most rainforest animals live in this layer.

Understorey
Shady, open area with young trees. Many insects live here.

Forest floor
Leaf litter is quickly eaten by insects.

The rainforest could vanish by 2030 unless its destruction is slowed down. Since 1800, half of it has been cut down for fuel, timber, and to make farmland, or has been lost through fire and drought.

Amazon forest being burned down to make farmland

Air plants

Air plants take in all the food and moisture they need from the air. They grow on trees high in the canopy. Some have leaves which cup water, helping them to survive dry spells.

Tadpoles in trees? Tree frogs lay their eggs in air-plant pools.

! The rainforest may only cover 6% of the Earth's land, but over 50% of all plant and animal species live there. One rainforest in Peru houses more types of bird than the whole of the USA.

Quetzals live in South American rainforests.

Ferns and mosses grow well in the warm, damp rainforest.

Healing herbs

Many medicines are made from rainforest plants. Quinine, the cure for malaria, comes from the cinchona tree. Over 70% of chemicals used to fight cancer come from the rainforest.

Rosy periwinkle – not just a pretty flower. It contains a chemical that fights cancer.

Rainforest record breakers

Smallest bird Bee hummingbird – 5.6cm long

Smallest deer Mouse deer – 50cm long, 25cm high

Largest rodent Capybara – 1m long, 60cm high

Largest frog Goliath frog – 40cm long

Largest snail African land snail – 25cm long

Largest spider Goliath birdeater – 25cm wide

Largest scorpion Emperor scorpion – 15cm long

Biggest butterfly Queen Alexandra's birdwing – 30cm wide

Largest centipede Peruvian giant centipede – 28cm long

Butterfly giant – Queen Alexandra's birdwing

Big stinkers

At 1m wide, the rafflesia is the world's biggest flower. It's amazing to see but not so great to sniff, as it smells of rotting meat. The smell attracts insects that spread the flower's pollen around the forest.

Rafflesia – stinking out the Malaysian rainforest.

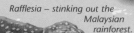

Rainforest crops

Materials	Gum, rubber
Timber	Mahogany, teak
Fruit	Bananas, pineapples
Spices	Paprika, pepper
Oils	Palm, patchouli
Fibres	Jute, rattan
Beans	Cocoa, coffee

Grasslands and Savannahs

About a quarter of the Earth's land is covered by huge expanses of grassy land called grasslands and savannahs. There is enough rain to stop this land turning to desert, but not enough for forests to grow.

Only patches of grass, scrub, bushes and a few trees grow on savannahs.

Grasslands have more grass and can be used for growing crops, such as wheat, or as pasture for grazing animals. Some grasses grow very tall.

Elephant grass grows up to 4.5m high in the savannah.

The map shows grassland regions: Prairie, Llanos, Steppes, Pampas, Campos, Savannah, Veldt, Scrub.

Grasslands and savannahs are known by different names in different regions.

Grassland	Name
Argentina	Pampas
North America	Prairie
South Africa	Veldt
Central Asia	Steppes
Australia	Scrub

Savannah	Name
East Africa	Savannah
Brazil	Campos
Venezuela	Llanos

Saiga antelope have inflatable noses. Their noses filter out dust in the dry summer months, and warm up cold air in winter.

This saiga antelope can blow its nose.

INTERNET LINKS
To find links to websites about grasslands and savannahs, go to **www.usborne-quicklinks.com**

Upside-down trees

African baobab trees have enormous, swollen trunks which store water for the dry season. Their branches are stumpy and look more like roots. Some old, hollow baobab trees have even been used as bus shelters or houses.

Baobab tree

Serious cereal

Cereal crops are wild grasses that have been cultivated by people. They are our main source of food. The pictures show the main crops and the number of tonnes harvested worldwide in 2002, starting with sugar cane, the biggest crop.

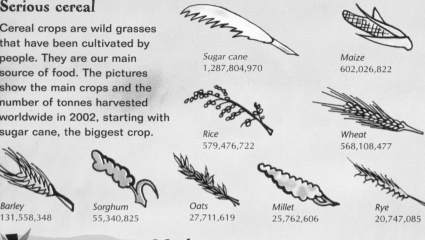

Sugar cane
1,287,804,970

Maize
602,026,822

Rice
579,476,722

Wheat
568,108,477

Barley
131,558,348

Sorghum
55,340,825

Oats
27,711,619

Millet
25,762,606

Rye
20,747,085

All the rice produced in the world in one day would make a pile the size of the Great Pyramid in Egypt.

Rice is the main food for over half the world. Over 90% of rice is grown in Asia.

Wind power

Grasses have flowers, but are not brightly coloured because they don't need to attract pollen-carrying insects. Wind carries their pollen from flower to flower.

There about 10,000 types of grass.

Now you see me

The colours of savannah predators help them to stalk their prey unseen. Striped or spotted animals, such as leopards and cheetahs, are hard to see from a distance. A lion's tawny colour hides it in the long, dry grass.

Watch out, there's a lion lying in wait in this long grass.

Grass gourmets

Grazing animals are very choosy about which part of a plant they eat. The same piece of grass may provide lunch for several different grazers.

Zebras nibble the tips, wildebeest munch the middle, and gazelle gobble the rest.

227

Deserts

One-fifth of the Earth's land is covered by desert. Only 15% of deserts are made up of sand, though. The rest are bare rock or have gravelly and pebbly surfaces. All deserts get less than 25cm of rainfall a year, so very little can grow there.

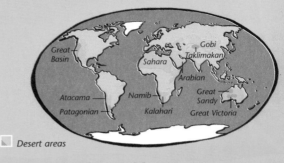

Desert areas

Great Sahara

The Sahara is the largest desert on Earth. It is about the size of the USA and covers over a third of Africa. Millions of years ago, it wasn't desert, but was covered in forests and grasslands teeming with wildlife.

Deserts of the world

Hot deserts are hot by day, all year round. Cold deserts have hot summers and cooler winters.

Desert	Location	Area (km²)	Type
Sahara	North Africa	9,100,000	Hot
Arabian	Saudi Arabia	2,300,000	Hot
Gobi	Mongolia/China	1,295,000	Cold
Patagonian	Argentina	673,000	Cold
Kalahari	Botswana	520,000	Hot
Taklimakan	Western China	349,400	Cold
Great Victoria	Western/South Australia	348,750	Hot
Great Sandy	Western Australia	267,250	Hot
Great Basin	USA	190,000	Cold
Atacama	Chile	140,000	Cold
Namib	Namibia	135,000	Cold

Aerial view of ancient riverbeds branching through the Sahara

Colossal cacti

Cacti are only found in American deserts. The tallest is the 19m cardón cactus of the Sonoran Desert, Mexico. It lives for hundreds of years.

Up to 90% of a cactus is water it stores for dry spells.

The Atacama Desert in Chile is the driest place on Earth. Parts of it had no rain for 400 years, from 1570 to 1971. In other parts it has never rained.

Atacama – as dry as it gets

Worn away

Desert winds can be tough on rocks. Soft rock is blasted away by sand carried on the wind. This is called erosion. Harder rock is left behind, sometimes revealing spectacular rock shapes.

This huge, balancing boulder was carved out by desert winds.

INTERNET LINKS
To find links to websites about deserts and desert life, go to **www.usborne-quicklinks.com**

Desert animal	Lives in	Survival skills
Fennec fox	Sahara	Large ears help it lose heat.
Jerboa	Sahara	Long hind legs help it jump away from predators.
Sidewinder (a snake)	USA	Lifts and loops its body sideways to reduce contact with the hot sand.
Arabian camel (dromedary)	Arabian desert	Hump stores fat, and can store water in its stomach for days.
Thorny devil (a lizard)	Australia	Grooves on its back collect and channel dew into its mouth.
Tadpole shrimp	Deserts worldwide	Eggs lie dried in sand for years, only hatching if rain comes.

 When a Texas horned lizard wants to hide itself against the desert soil, it can make itself lighter or darker. If predators attack, it has one more trick – it squirts blood from its eyes.

Creeping dunes

Some sand dunes move. Wind blowing up one side blows sand down the other. Dunes creep forward 10-50m a year, sometimes covering villages and oases.

The Sossusvlei dunes in the Namib Desert are some of the world's highest – up to 300m.

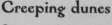

Mirages

Hot deserts are famous for mirages: tricks of the light that make pools of water seem to appear, then vanish as you get closer to them. You might see the same effect on roads on hot days.

How mirages work

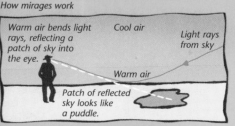

Warm air bends light rays, reflecting a patch of sky into the eye.

Cool air

Light rays from sky

Warm air

Patch of reflected sky looks like a puddle.

An inviting pool in the desert? No – it's a mirage.

Lakes and Rivers

Only 3% of Earth's water is fresh – the rest is salty. Two-thirds of fresh water is frozen in ice sheets and glaciers. Most of the little that remains is in lakes, rivers and under the ground.

Continent	Longest river	Length
Africa	Nile	6,671km
South America	Amazon	6,440km
Asia	Chang Jiang (Yangtze)	6,380km
North America	Mississippi-Missouri-Red Rock	6,019km
Oceania	Murray-Darling	3,718km
Europe	Volga	3,700km

Deep in Siberia

The world's deepest lake is also the oldest. Lake Baikal in Siberia, Russia, is over 1.6km at its deepest point and contains one-fifth of all the world's fresh water. It is 25 million years old.

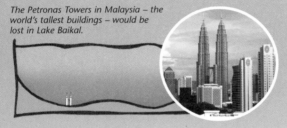

The Petronas Towers in Malaysia – the world's tallest buildings – would be lost in Lake Baikal.

! The largest freshwater fish is the wels catfish* (the record is 5m long). These giants were brought to the UK by landowners in the 1800s, thinking they would be good to eat, but they proved hard to catch. Some still lurk in British lakes today, even preying on ducks.

Going nowhere

Not all rivers flow to the sea — some disappear. The Okavango, in Botswana, Africa, fans out into a mass of streams and swampland 15,500km² in area. Its waters finally vanish into the Kalahari Desert.

Largest lakes and inland seas	Location	Area
Caspian Sea	Western Asia	370,999km²
Lake Superior	USA/Canada	82,414km²
Lake Victoria	Tanzania/Uganda	69,215km²
Lake Huron	USA/Canada	59,596km²
Lake Michigan	USA	58,016km²
Lake Tanganyika	Tanzania/Congo	32,764km²
Lake Baikal	Russia	31,500km²

*The Beluga sturgeon is bigger, up to 8m long, but it lives mainly at sea.

Highest waterfalls	Location	Height
Angel Falls	Venezuela	979m
Tugela Falls	South Africa	948m
Kjelsfossen	Norway	840m
Mtarazi	Zimbabwe	762m
Yosemite Falls	USA	739m
Mongefoss	Norway	714m
Espelandsfoss	Norway	703m

INTERNET LINKS
To find links to websites about lakes and rivers,
go to **www.usborne-quicklinks.com**

Amazing Amazon

The river that carries most water is the Amazon. Starting 5,200m up in the Andes, it ends on the Atlantic coast in a maze of islands and channels 300km wide. Its silty, yellow-brown fresh water flows 180km out to sea.

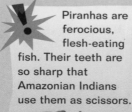

Piranhas are ferocious, flesh-eating fish. Their teeth are so sharp that Amazonian Indians use them as scissors.

Floating islands

Titicaca, 3,810m up in the Peruvian Andes, is the world's highest sailable lake. Floating on it are islands, some as big as football fields, made from matted reeds. Uros Indians make the islands and live on them. They also build their houses and boats from the reeds.

A Uros reed boat on Lake Titicaca

Moving falls

The force of the Niagara Falls slowly grinds away the rocks at its edge, causing the Falls to move. Today, the Falls are midway along the Niagara River, on the Canada-USA border between Lake Ontario and Lake Erie. 10,000 years ago, the Falls were 11km further downstream.

The Falls 10,000 years ago

Niagara Falls today

In 25,000 years, the Falls will vanish as they reach Lake Erie.

The Seashore

If all the world's coastlines were stretched out end to end, they would measure 504,000km – long enough to go around the Earth 13 times.

INTERNET LINKS
To find links to websites about the seashore, go to www.usborne-quicklinks.com

Highest sea cliffs

North America

Molokai, Hawaii	1,010m

South America

Coastal Range, N. Chile	1,000m

Asia

Chingshui Cliffs, Taiwan	760m

Europe

Enniberg, Faroe Islands	754m

Oceania

Port Arthur, Tasmania	300m

Africa

Cape Point, South Africa	249m

Changing coast

The coastline can change position over a long period of time. Many ancient Roman ports around the Mediterranean Sea, such as Caesarea on the coast of Israel, are now underwater. By contrast, on England's south coast, the old port of Rye, in Sussex, is now 3km inland.

Rye 250 years ago

Rye today

Rising tide

The sea rises and falls on the shore twice a day, at high and low tides. The biggest difference in tides is in the Bay of Fundy, Canada, where high tide reaches 16m.

Stormy weather

In winter, waves crash onto the northern shores of the Pacific Ocean with the same force as a car hitting a wall at 145kph. Storm waves on the west coast of North America once tossed a rock weighing 61kg, the weight of a grown person, 28m up onto the roof of a lighthouse.

Portland Head in Maine, USA, is made of tough rock that has resisted storms for hundreds of years.

Wearing and grinding

Sand is made from rock that is worn down as it is washed out to sea by rivers, or ground down by waves battering cliffs. Some beaches have sand of one colour, such as the black lava stone beaches of Tahiti. Others are a mixture of colours, made from various rocks, worn-down coral, or seashells.

Sand colour	Made from
Black	Lava stone
Grey	Granite, feldspar
Tan	Granite, quartz
Yellow	Quartz
Gold	Mica
Red	Garnet
Pink	Feldspar
White	Coral, seashells, quartz
Green	Olivine

 The coast at Martha's Vineyard, in Massachussets, USA, is worn away so quickly by waves – 1.7m each year – that a lighthouse standing there has had to be moved inland three times.

Here we go again...

Towering dunes

Some sand dunes on France's Atlantic coast reach an amazing 108m high – seven times higher than most beach dunes. The dunes, blown by wind, creep slowly inland by about 6m a year. They may bury buildings and even whole forests.

The enormous Dune of Pilat at Arcachon on France's west coast

Rock carving

Coastlines are always changing. On rocky shores, waves pound against the cliffs, flinging up boulders, pebbles and sand. These grind away the rock, forming headlands, caves, arches and stacks.

Headland

Sea cave

Arch

Stack

The Ocean

Two-thirds of Earth's surface is covered by salt water. It is divided into five oceans but they are all connected. The largest ocean is the Pacific. At its widest point (between Panama and Malaysia) it stretches for 17,700km – nearly halfway around the world.

Earth's oceans	Area
Pacific Ocean	155,557,000km²
Atlantic Ocean	76,762,000km²
Indian Ocean	68,556,000km²
Southern Ocean	20,327,000km²
Arctic Ocean	14,056,000km²

1 Pacific Ocean
2 Atlantic Ocean
3 Indian Ocean
4 Southern Ocean
5 Arctic Ocean

Most whale sounds are too low for us to hear.

Oceans and seas

Parts of the Earth's five oceans are divided into areas called seas.

Largest seas	Area	Ocean
Weddell Sea	8,000,000km²	Southern
Arabian Sea	7,456,000km²	Indian
South China Sea	2,974,000km²	Pacific
Mediterranean Sea	2,505,000km²	Atlantic
Barents Sea	1,300,000km²	Arctic

Whalesongs

Sound travels through water over four times as quickly as it does through air. Low-pitched whalesongs can carry for hundreds of kilometres under the sea. Whales may sing to attract a distant mate.

The surface of the Moon has been much more thoroughly explored than the deep oceans of our own planet.

We call the dark patches on the Moon seas and oceans, but they are as dry as dust.

Cucumber city

Thousands of sea cucumbers – simple animals related to sea urchins – live deep in trenches in the seabed. If you weighed all the animals that live on the seabed, about 95% of their combined weight would be made up of sea cucumbers.

Sea cucumber – animal not vegetable

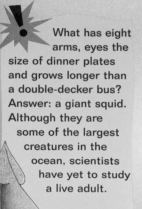

What has eight arms, eyes the size of dinner plates and grows longer than a double-decker bus? Answer: a giant squid. Although they are some of the largest creatures in the ocean, scientists have yet to study a live adult.

Would you like to wrestle with an animal whose eyes were bigger than your head?

Deeply fishy

Most plants and animals only live at particular depths of the ocean. Many fish are coloured to make them hard to see at their depth.

Surface *Masses of tiny floating plants and animals, called plankton. Fish living here are often blue, green or violet.*

Herring

Mackerel

Squid

100m *Plants don't grow far below 100m, as there is little light.*

 Hatchet fish

Tuna

200m *In the "twilight zone", most fish are pale or silvery*

Jellyfish

Great white shark

Deep-sea eel

1000m *In the dark depths, fish are mostly black, or dark-coloured. Some creatures are bright red, as red light can't reach these depths, making them nearly invisible.*

Lantern fish

Many deep-sea animals have lights on their bodies.

Angler fish

4000m *Over half of the ocean bed lies at 4,000m or deeper.*

Undersea landscape

If the oceans were drained away, an amazing landscape would be revealed. Running through the Atlantic Ocean is the world's longest mountain range: the Mid-Atlantic Ridge. Lying between Japan and New Guinea is the Mariana Trench – a valley that plunges 11km down to the deepest point on Earth.

INTERNET LINKS
To find links to websites about seas and oceans, and ocean life, go to
www.usborne-quicklinks.com

A 3-D map of part of the Mid-Atlantic Ridge

235

Poles Apart

The North Pole is in the middle of the huge Arctic ice cap, which floats on the Arctic Ocean. There is no land there.

The Arctic   Ice cap

Arctic facts

Area of ice	10,000,000km² (permanent) 14,090,000km² (winter)
Ice cap thickness	Up to 1.5km
Sea ice thickness	3m (average)
Arctic Ocean depth	1,300m (average); 5,450m (greatest)
Area of Greenland ice sheet	1,479,000km²
Thickness of Greenland ice	1.6–3km
Temperature at North Pole	-32°C (average)
North Pole first reached by	Robert Peary and Matthew Henson (USA), 1909
Nearest Settlement to Pole	Siorapaluk, Greenland
Examples of wildlife	Polar bear, snowy owl, Arctic fox, walrus, common seal, hooded seal

"Green" land

Greenland – Earth's largest island – is not very green. 85% of it is covered in ice. It was named by an early settler, Eric the Red, who was trying to persuade fellow Vikings to come and join him.

In 1958, the first nuclear submarine, *USS Nautilus*, became the first vessel to travel directly under the North Pole.

USS Nautilus in New York

Flooded cities

The polar ice sheets hold over 2% of Earth's water. If they melted, the sea level would rise by over 60m. Many coastal areas and major cities would be drowned.

Europe if the ice sheets melted

☐ Underwater   ☐ Dry land

Hunt the seal

Arctic seals need to come up for air every 20 minutes. When the seas are frozen, the seals chew big breathing holes in the ice.

Polar bears hunt seals, waiting patiently by the breathing holes. When a seal comes up for air, the bear grabs it.

An Arctic seal takes its last breath.

INTERNET LINKS
To find links to websites about the Poles, go to
www.usborne-quicklinks.com

White land

Antarctica is land, but is covered in glaciers that hold 90% of all the ice on Earth.

Antarctica

■ Ice cap   ■ Ice shelf

Roald the bold

In 1911, the trailblazing Norwegian explorer, Roald Amundsen, was the first person to reach the South Pole. Fifteen years later, with the Italian Umberto Nobile, he flew on the first airship over the North Pole.

Roald Amundsen

Antarctic facts

Area of ice	4,000,000km² (permanent) 21,000,000km² (winter)
Ice cap thickness	Up to 4km
Sea ice thickness	4m (average)
Southern Ocean depth	4,200m (average); 7,235m (greatest)
Temperature at South Pole	-50°C (average)
South Pole first reached by	Roald Amundsen (Norway), 1911
Nearest settlement to Pole	No permanent Antarctic settlements
Examples of wildlife	Penguin, blue whale, elephant seal, albatross, Weddell seal, leopard seal

Deep water

Lake Vostok is a massive, prehistoric lake sealed 3.6km beneath the ice of east Antarctica, the coldest place on Earth (-89.2°C). Scientists think its water is kept liquid by heat from inside the Earth.

Antarctica is a desert. Inland, less than 5cm of new snow falls in a year. Most of the snow blowing around there has been lifted and shifted by winds.

The shadowy shape of a lake deep beneath the Antarctic ice

Antarctica, 2,400m above sea level on average, is the highest continent. It is split in two by the Transantarctic Mountains (below), one of the longest mountain ranges in the world.

Glaciers and Icebergs

Glaciers are masses of ice that move slowly down mountains or through valleys. They cover a tenth of Earth's dry surface.

Continent	Longest glacier	Length
Antarctica	Lambert-Fisher glacier	515km
Europe	Novaya Zemlya glacier, Russia	418km
North America	Bering glacier, Alaska	204km
Asia	Biafao-Hispar glacier, Pakistan	125km
South America	Upsala glacier, Andes, Chile	60km
Oceania	Tasman glacier, New Zealand	29km
Africa	Credner glacier, Kilimanjaro, Tanzania	1km

Birth of a berg

A glacier's melting end is called its snout. Icebergs are made, or "calved", when pieces of the glacier break off the snout into the sea.

Pacier glacier

Most glaciers creep slowly down mountains, at 3–60cm a day, but the fastest, the Columbia glacier in Alaska, moves up to 35m every day.

Icebergs being calved from Margerie Glacier in Glacier Bay, Alaska, USA

Deep freeze

In 1820, three climbers died when they fell into a crack in a glacier on Mon Blanc in the Alps. Forty-o years later, their bodies emerged, well-preserved, from the glacier's melting snout. Cracks in glaciers are called crevasses and can be 40m deep.

Mind the gap!

Tropical ice

Glaciers are even found near the equator, on mountains over 6,000m high. There is glacier ice 60m deep on Mount Kilimanjaro in Tanzania.

! 75% of all the fresh water on Earth is frozen in glaciers. That's the equivalent of 60 years of non-stop rain.

Biggest berg

The largest iceberg ever recorded was 31,000km² in area – that's slightly larger than Belgium. It was seen off the Antarctic coast in 1956.

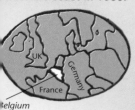

Tallest berg

The tallest iceberg ever seen, off west Greenland, was 167m high – one and a half times as tall as the Eiffel Tower in Paris.

Hidden depths

Only one-eighth of an iceberg shows above the water. If, for example, the iceberg that sank the *Titanic* had shown 30m above the water, then there must have been another 210m below.

The tip of the iceberg is only a fraction of what lies beneath.

One Arctic iceberg drifted 4,000km, nearly as far south as Bermuda. An Antarctic iceberg drifted for 5,500km, nearly as far north as Rio de Janeiro in Brazil.

Big icebergs can drift a very long way before melting.

Iceberg ahoy!

The International Ice Patrol keeps track of icebergs in the North Atlantic, warning ships of any danger. The Patrol was set up after the great liner *RMS Titanic* sank after hitting an iceberg on April 14, 1912. Over 1,500 people drowned.

The biggest icebergs are in Antarctica. Can you spot the penguins?

Iceberg classes	Height above sea level	Length
Growler	under 1m	under 5m
Bergy bit	1-5m	5-15m
Small iceberg	5-15m	16-60m
Medium iceberg	16-45m	61-120m
Large iceberg	46-75m	121-200m
Very large iceberg	over 75m	over 200m

Iceberg shapes

Tabular

Dome

Pinnacle

Blocky

Wedge

Drydock

INTERNET LINKS
To find links to the coolest ice websites, go to **www.usborne-quicklinks.com**

239

Natural Resources

We use resources from the Earth to give us energy for heat and light. The chart below shows how much of the energy we use comes from natural resources. Renewable resources are those that can be reused or regrown.

Resource	Origin	% of world energy	Renewable
Oil	Underground, undersea	34.8%	✗
Coal	Underground	23.5%	✗
Natural gas	Underground	21.1%	✗
Wood and waste	Trees, industry, households	11.0%	✓
Nuclear power	Energy released from atoms	6.8%	✗
Hydropower	Rivers and waterfalls	2.3%	✓
Geothermal	Underground hot water/steam	0.44%	✓
Solar	Energy from sunlight	0.04%	✓
Wind	Wind energy	0.03%	✓
Tidal	Wave energy	0.004%	✓

The Sun gives warmth and light that can be changed into electricity.

Fossil fools?

Fossil fuels (oil, coal and gas) were made from the remains of plants and animals buried beneath the sea millions of years ago. Some day, fossil fuels will run out. At the rate we are using them, we may see oil shortages by 2020, and run low on gas by 2040. Coal may last until 2200.

The remains of prehistoric plants can be seen in these lumps of coal.

INTERNET LINKS
To find links to websites about the world's natural resources, go to **www.usborne-quicklinks.com**

Well, well...

About a third of the world's oil comes from undersea oil wells. A North Sea oil platform can produce 8,000,000 litres of oil a day. That would fill eight Olympic-sized swimming pools.

Under 5% of the world's population live in the USA, but they use more than 25% of the world's oil and electricity.

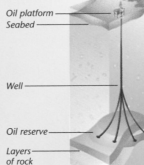

Oil platform
Seabed
Well
Oil reserve
Layers of rock

Sunny side up

The Sun is the biggest energy source we have: in one hour it beams more energy to Earth, in the form of sunlight, than the world uses in a year. The Sun's energy can be collected using solar panels. In places with no mains electricity – parts of Kenya, Africa, for example – many homes power lamps, radios and TVs with solar panels on their roofs.

This house runs on sunshine.

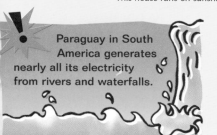

Paraguay in South America generates nearly all its electricity from rivers and waterfalls.

Hydropower

Over a sixth of the world's electricity is generated by the force of water. Electricity generated by water flowing in rivers and over waterfalls is called hydropower.

Country	% of world hydropower
Canada	13.2%
Brazil	11.3%
USA	10.2%
China	8.2%
Russia	6.1%
Norway	5.2%
Japan	3.6%
Sweden	2.9%
India	2.7%
France	2.7%

Staying warm in Iceland

In Iceland, water that's been warmed inside the Earth is used to heat buildings and even open-air swimming pools. It is also piped under the ground to melt snow and ice. In winter, 2,300 litres of naturally boiling water is pumped into the capital city, Reykjavik, every second.

Water heated by this geothermal** power station in Iceland is used as an open-air swimming pool.

Oil products	**Coal products**
Petrol (gasoline)	Plastics
Diesel fuel	Heavy chemicals*
Kerosene (jet fuel)	Perfumes
Plastics	Insecticides
Paraffin wax	Antiseptics
Medicines	Road surfaces
Explosives	Coal gas
Pesticides	
Detergents	*Many things we use are made from oil and coal.*
Cosmetics	
Paints	

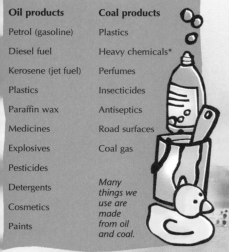

* Chemicals used in bulk in industry and farming
**Geothermal energy: Earth's natural heat energy

Earth's Problems

Most of the Earth's problems are caused by humans. We are using up fossil fuels and spoiling land, polluting air and water, and even changing the weather along the way.

Global warming

The world is getting warmer. Many scientists think the large amount of carbon dioxide gas made by burning fossil fuels is partly to blame.

Coal-fired power station, UK

Trees soak up carbon dioxide, using it to grow, but the destruction of the rainforest means there are fewer trees to do this.

Problems caused by global warming

- Storms and floods
- Deadly heatwaves
- Droughts and forest fires
- Loss of the northern forests
- Spread of disease-carrying insects
- Shifting seasons confusing wildlife
- Melting glaciers and rising sea-level

Gone forever

Animal species die out naturally over time, but many are now becoming extinct extremely quickly.

Scientists think that by 2030 nearly a quarter of mammal species might have disappeared.

There are only about 7,000 tigers left in the wild.

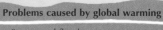

Mammals in danger	Number in wild	Threats
Amur leopard	55	Hunted for fur; used in traditional medicine
Javan rhino	60	Homes destroyed by logging; hunted for horns
Baiji dolphin	150	Water pollution
Wild bactrian camel	350	Hunted for meat; seen as competition with livestock
Silvery gibbon	400	Homes destroyed by logging and clearing for farmland

There are six billion people on Earth. By 2030, there could be eight billion – a third as many again. There is space on Earth for them all, but sharing food and fuel fairly will be a huge challenge.

Mining

Mining for minerals can spoil massive areas of land and cause pollution. Poisonous waste from mining can wash into rivers, killing wildlife and giving people health problems. Mining is also very dangerous: 40 miners are killed each day, on average.

Water waste

Of the 90 million tonnes of fish taken from the oceans each year, a quarter are thrown back, unwanted. Most of these die. Some species, such as Atlantic cod, have nearly been wiped out in this way.

We don't just take from the ocean, though: each year we dump 6.4 million tonnes of rubbish into it.

Nets with large holes let young fish go free.

Every year, an area of the world's forest larger than Hungary is chopped down.

Factory waste oozing into a river

Environmental disasters

Oil-soaked guillemot

Date	Location	Disaster
2002	Galicia, Spain	The *Prestige* oil spill. Over 900km of coastline polluted, and thousands of sea birds affected
2001	Galápagos islands	The *Jessica* oil spill. Many marine iguanas killed by oil pollution
1991	Kuwait	Oil fields set alight during the Gulf War, leading to air pollution and acid rain
1989	Alaska, USA	The *Exxon Valdez* oil spill. Many thousands of sea birds and animals killed by oil slick
1986	Chernobyl, Ukraine	Explosion of nuclear reactor. Thousands killed or damaged by radiation-related diseases
1984	Bhopal, India	Poison gas tank explosion. Over 8,000 people killed; thousands more disabled and injured

Uprooted

Forests act as a barrier to wind and water. Where trees are cut down, winds and floods can sweep away the soil, making the ground useless for growing anything at all.

Treeless land is unprotected.

Water woes

A fifth of all people don't have enough clean water to drink. Two-fifths have nowhere clean to go to the toilet.

Causes of water problems

- Rivers and seas polluted by chemical waste from factories

- Wasteful crop-watering methods

- Drought caused by global warming

- More people sharing water resources

Young girls collecting water from holes dug in the ground in Udaipur, India

INTERNET LINKS
To find links to websites about Planet Earth's problems, go to
www.usborne-quicklinks.com

Finding Solutions

Earth may have many problems, but it also has many people who are trying to solve them. Here are a few ways we can tackle some of Earth's problems.

Terrific terraces

Building terraces can stop heavy rain washing away soil from mountain slopes. For example, three rice crops a year can be grown on some terraces in Bali.

Rice has been farmed on terraces in Bali for hundreds of years.

Recycling

Many everyday items can be recycled. Here are just a few.

Cardboard boxes

Clothes

Electrical goods

Furniture

Glass jars and bottles

Magazines and papers

Metal drinks cans

Plastic bottles

Vegetable waste can be made into compost

This jacket began life as 25 plastic bottles.

Healthy mix

Soil can be made more fertile by growing different crops together, rather than only one. In Java, pineapples and winged beans are grown in alternate rows, which keeps the soil fertile.

Mixed crops keep soil tip-top.

Saving water

70% of the water we use in the world is used for watering crops. Spraying crops with water in hot areas is very wasteful because so much dries up in the Sun's heat.

A huge amount can be saved by giving plants small measures of water through holes in thin plastic tubes in the soil.

A wasteful way to water crops

Wind power

Electricity can be generated by wind turbines, rather than by burning fossil fuels in power stations.

If wind turbines were set up in the choppy seas around Great Britain, they could supply three times the power Britain uses today.

Just one wind turbine can supply the energy needs of 1,000 homes.

INTERNET LINKS
To find links to websites about solving world problems, go to
www.usborne-quicklinks.com

Tree bombs

One solution to the loss of forests is the amazing idea of dropping "tree bombs" from planes.

Stand clear!

Treeless areas could be bombed with thousands of saplings in cone-shaped capsules which would then rot and bed the trees into the earth.

Coral reefs shelter a huge range of sealife and are a barrier against strong waves.

In Japan and China, thousands of ducks are used, instead of dangerous chemicals, to control insects that attack rice fields. A duck can eat 2kg of insect pests a day.

Duck after a day's work

Sweet fuel

Many cars in Brazil run on fuel mixed with ethanol, made from sugar cane. Using ethanol causes less pollution than petrol.

Being prepared

Global warming* already seems to be bringing more natural disasters. Below are some actions that can be taken to reduce their effects.

Replant forests to protect soil from storms and floods

Use sensors and satellites to watch for early signs of disasters such as hurricanes

Limit the use of water, to protect against drought

Protect coral reefs, which defend shorelines from violent waves

*See page 242

Times and Seasons

The lengths of our days and years come from the time it takes the Earth to turn and to travel around the Sun.

Years and years

A year is the time it takes for the Earth to circle the Sun once. In the Gregorian calendar, a year has 365 days, but it actually takes the Earth 365.24 days to complete its circle.

To keep the calendar in step with the Sun, every fourth year has an extra day: February 29. These are called leap years. The maths still doesn't quite add up, though, so a leap year falling on a century is only counted as a leap year every 400 years.

INTERNET LINKS
To find links to websites about Earth's times and seasons, go to **www.usborne-quicklinks.com**

In each journey around the Sun, the Earth travels 940,000,000km.

Day and night

A day is the time it takes the Earth to spin once around on its axis: 24 hours. The half of the Earth facing the Sun has its daytime while the other half has its night.

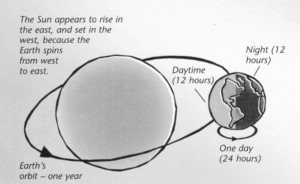

The Sun appears to rise in the east, and set in the west, because the Earth spins from west to east.

Night (12 hours)

Daytime (12 hours)

One day (24 hours)

Earth's orbit – one year

World calendars

Gregorian	Days	Jewish	Days	Islamic	Days	Indian	Days
Sun-based		*Sun- and Moon-based*		*Moon-based**		*Sun-based***	
January	31	Tishri (Sep-Oct)	30	Muharram	30	Chaitra (Mar-Apr)	30/31
February	28/29	Heshvan (Oct-Nov)	29/30	Safar	29	Vaishakha (Apr-May)	31
March	31	Kislev (Nov-Dec)	29/30	Rabi 1	30	Jyeshtha (May-Jun)	31
April	30	Tevet (Dec-Jan)	29	Rabi 2	29	Asadha (Jun-Jul)	31
May	31	Shevat (Jan-Feb)	30	Jumada 1	30	Shravana (Jul-Aug)	31
June	30	Adar 1 (Feb-Mar)	29	Jumada 2	29	Bhadra (Aug-Sep)	31
July	31	Adar 2 (in leap year)	30	Rajab	30	Ashvija (Sep-Oct)	30
August	31	Nisan (Mar-Apr)	30	Shaban	29	Kartika (Oct-Nov)	30
September	30	Iyar (Apr-May)	29	Ramadan	30	Agrahayana (Nov-Dec)	30
October	31	Sivan (May-Jun)	30	Shawwal	29	Pushya (Dec-Jan)	30
November	30	Tammuz (Jun-Jul)	29	Dhu al-Qadah	30	Magha (Jan-Feb)	30
December	31	Av (Jul-Aug)	30	Dhu al-Hijjah	29/30	Phalguna (Feb-Mar)	30
		Elul (Aug-Sep)	29				

* Being timed by moon cycles alone, Islamic months do not tie in with Gregorian months.
**This is the National Calendar of India. India also uses other Sun- and Moon-based calendars.

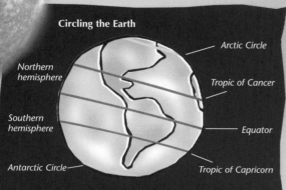

Circling the Earth

Arctic Circle

Northern hemisphere

Tropic of Cancer

Southern hemisphere

Equator

Antarctic Circle

Tropic of Capricorn

Equator Imaginary circle around the middle of the Earth

Northern hemisphere Half of the Earth north of the equator

Southern hemisphere Half of the Earth south of the equator

Arctic Circle Circle inside which the Sun can be seen at midnight on the June solstice

Antarctic Circle Circle inside which the Sun can be seen at midnight on the December solstice

Tropic of Cancer Most northerly circle at which Sun is overhead in northern summer

Tropic of Capricorn Most southerly circle at which Sun is overhead in southern summer

Be sure to pack your sunglasses if you're visiting the Arctic Circle this summer, because the Sun never sets during the summer months. The area inside the Circle is called the Land of the Midnight Sun.

Another sunny summer night in the Arctic circle...

The seasons

The Earth is tilted at an angle. As it travels around the Sun, some parts of it get more direct sunlight than others. This makes the seasons change.

At the June solstice, when the Sun is overhead at the Tropic of Cancer, summer starts in the northern hemisphere and winter starts in the southern hemisphere. In December, the opposite happens.

At the equinoxes, the Sun is overhead at the equator. Neither hemisphere is then warmer than the other, and the milder seasons of spring and autumn begin.

Key
- Sun overhead
- Most direct sunlight
- Spring starts
- Summer starts
- Autumn starts
- Winter starts

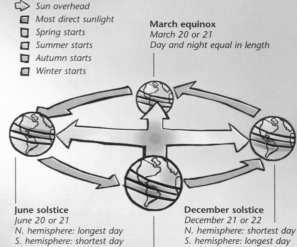

March equinox
March 20 or 21
Day and night equal in length

June solstice
June 20 or 21
N. hemisphere: longest day
S. hemisphere: shortest day

December solstice
December 21 or 22
N. hemisphere: shortest day
S. hemisphere: longest day

September equinox
September 22 or 23
Day and night equal in length

World Records

This map shows where some of the highest, deepest, largest and longest features of Planet Earth are.

Largest continent
Asia: 44,537,920km²

Deepest lake
Lake Baikal, Siberia, Russia: 1,642m

Deepest cave
Gouffre Mirolda/ Lucien Bouclier, France: 1,733m

Largest inland sea
Caspian Sea: 370,999km²

Deepest valley
Yarlung Tsangpo Gorge, China: 5,075m

Highest mountain on land
Everest, Nepal/ China: 8,850m

Highest tsunami
Ishigaki Island, Japan, 1771: 85m

Deepest part of ocean
Challenger Deep, Mariana Trench: 11,022m

Hottest temperature ever
El Azizia, Libya, 1922: 58°C.

Red Sea

Longest river
Nile, Africa: 6,671km

Earth's lowest point
Dead Sea, Israel/ Jordan: 411m below sea level

Longest valley system
Great Rift Valley: 4,800km

Largest bay (by area)
Bay of Bengal: 2,172,000km²

The Red Sea is a flooded part of the world's largest valley – the Great Rift Valley. The valley runs for over 4,800km, from Mozambique to Syria. It formed where two faults in the Earth run side by side, and the land between has sunk.

Longest glacier
Lambert-Fisher glacier, East Antarctica: 515km

Coldest temperature ever
Vostok, East Antarctica, 1983: -89.2°C.

Largest ocean
Pacific Ocean:
155,557,000km²

Largest island
Greenland:
2,175,600km²

Longest fjord
Nordvest Fjord,
Scoresby Sund,
Greenland:
313km

**Largest bay
(by shoreline)**
Hudson Bay,
Canada: 12,268km

Highest geyser
Service Steamboat
Geyser, Yellowstone,
USA: 115m max.

Largest lake
Lake Superior,
USA/Canada:
82,414km²

Highest tide
Bay of Fundy, Nova
Scotia, Canada:
rises over 15m

**Highest
cliffs**
Molokai,
Hawaii
1,005m

Longest canyon
Grand Canyon,
Arizona, USA: 349km

Longest cave system
Mammoth Caves,
Kentucky, USA: 484km

Highest mountain on Earth
Mauna Kea, Hawaii: 10,203m
measured from seabed

Largest gulf
Gulf of Mexico:
1,544,000km²

Highest waterfall
Angel Falls,
Venezuela: 979m

**Highest seamount
(underwater volcano)**
near Tonga Trench:
8,690m

**Longest
mountain range**
Andes, South
America: 7,240km

Highest active volcano
Ojos del Salado, Chile/
Argentina: 6,887m

River carrying most water
Amazon, South America:
180,000m³ flows into the
Atlantic Ocean every second.

INTERNET LINKS
To find links to websites about Earth's amazing
features, go to **www.usborne-quicklinks.com**

249

Glossary

Arctic Circle The parallel (66°34′N) that circles the cold regions around the North Pole. In the northern summer the Sun never sets north of it.

Antarctic Circle The parallel (66°34′S) that circles the cold regions around the South Pole. In the southern summer the Sun never sets south of it.

atmosphere A blanket of gases around a planet.

axis An imaginary line through the Earth around which it spins.

continental plate A tectonic plate supporting a land mass.

continents Earth's great land masses: Asia, Africa, North and South America, Europe, Oceania (includes Australia) and Antarctica.

crust Earth's rocky outermost layer.

current A band of water running through the ocean.

degree (°) Unit used to measure distance around the Earth as an angle of latitude or longitude.

equator An imaginary circle, at 0° latitude, which divides the Earth into the northern and southern hemispheres.

equinoxes Days in March and September when the Sun is overhead at the equator and day and night are equal in length.

erosion The process by which rock is worn down by wind and water.

geologist A scientist who studies Earth's history, structure and rocks.

hemisphere Half of the Earth, for example, the southern hemisphere.

International Date Line The meridian opposite the prime meridian. It snakes around 180° longitude, to avoid land. Places west of the line are a day ahead of those east of it.

latitude Distance north or south, measured as an angle in degrees (°) from the equator.

lava Liquid rock above the Earth's surface.

lithosphere Earth's outer shell, made up of the crust and upper mantle.

longitude Distance east or west, measured as an angle in degrees (°) from the prime meridian.

magma Liquid rock under the Earth's surface.

magnetic poles The two points on Earth's surface between which compass needles line up.

mantle A hot, slowly shifting rock layer between the Earth's crust and core.

meridians (lines of longitude) Imaginary lines joining the Earth's poles

oceanic plate An undersea tectonic plate.

parallels (lines of latitude) Imaginary circles around the Earth in line with the equator.

poles Earth's geographic poles are the points at each end of its axis.

prime meridian The meridian at 0° longitude, which passes through Greenwich, England.

seamount A volcano beneath the sea.

seaquake An undersea earthquake.

solstices Days in June and December when the midday Sun is overhead at one of the Tropics.

spreading ridge An undersea mountain range formed when lava rises to fill cracks in the seabed.

subduction zone A place where two plates collide and one plate moves beneath the other.

tectonic plate A large piece of the Earth's lithosphere.

trench A deep, V-shaped dip in the seabed, formed at a subduction zone.

Tropic of Cancer The most northerly parallel (23°26′N) at which the Sun is overhead in the northern summer.

Tropic of Capricorn The most southerly parallel (23°26′S) at which the Sun is overhead in the southern summer.

Using the Internet

Internet links

Most of the websites described in this book can be accessed with a standard home computer and an Internet browser (the software that enables you to display information from the Internet). We recommend:

• A PC with Microsoft® Windows 98 or later version, or a Macintosh computer with System 9.0 or later, and 64Mb RAM
• A browser such as Microsoft® Internet Explorer 5, or Netscape® 6, or later versions
• Connection to the Internet via a modem (preferably 56Kbps) or a faster digital or cable line
• An account with an Internet Service Provider (ISP)
• A sound card to hear sound files

Extras

Some websites need additional free programs, called plug-ins, to play sounds, or to show videos, animations or 3-D images. If you go to a site and you do not have the necessary plug-in, a message saying so will come up on the screen. There is usually a button on the site that you can click on to download the plug-in. Alternatively, go to **www.usborne-quicklinks.com** and click on **Net Help**. There you can find links to download plug-ins. Here is a list of plug-ins you might need:

RealOne™ Player – lets you play videos and hear sound files
QuickTime – lets you view video clips
Shockwave® – lets you play animations and interactive programs
Flash™ – lets you play animations

Help

For general help and advice on using the Internet, go to **Usborne Quicklinks** at **www.usborne-quicklinks.com** and click on **Net Help**. To find out more about how to use your web browser, click on **Help** at the top of the browser, and then choose Contents and Index. You'll find a huge searchable dictionary containing tips on how to find your way around the Internet.

Internet safety

Remember to follow the Internet safety guidelines at the front of this book. For more safety information, go to **Usborne Quicklinks** and click on **Net Help**.

Computer viruses

A computer virus is a program that can seriously damage your computer. A virus can get into your computer when you download programs from the Internet, or in an attachment (an extra file) that arrives with an email. We strongly recommend that you buy anti-virus software to protect your computer, and that you update the software regularly.

INTERNET LINK
To find a link to a website where you can find out more about computer viruses, go to **www.usborne-quicklinks.com** and click on **Net Help**.

Macintosh and QuickTime are trademarks of Apple Computer, Inc., registered in the U.S. and other countries.
RealOne Player is a trademark of RealNetworks, Inc., registered in the U.S. and other countries.
Flash and Shockwave are trademarks of Macromedia, Inc., registered in the U.S. and other countries.

Index

Acknowledgements

Every effort has been made to trace the copyright holders of the material in this book. If any rights have been omitted, the publishers offer to rectify this in any subsequent editions following notification. The publishers are grateful to the following organizations and individuals for their permission to reproduce material (t=top, m=middle, b=bottom, l=left, r=right):

Corbis: 193 Royalty-Free/CORBIS; 198 Myron Jay Dorf/CORBIS; 199 Bill Ross/CORBIS; 202br Dewitt Jones/ CORBIS; 204 S. P. Gillette/CORBIS; 207br Tom Bean/CORBIS; 212m Charles O'Rear/CORBIS; 213m Bettmann/ CORBIS, 213b Roger Ressmeyer/CORBIS; 214b Roger Ressmeyer/CORBIS; 216 Galen Rowell/ CORBIS; 217 James Sparshatt/CORBIS; 221ml Darrell Gulin/CORBIS; 230m Graham Tim/CORBIS SYGMA; 231b Nevada Weir/CORBIS; 233bm Frederik Astier/CORBIS SYGMA; 237ml Bettmann/CORBIS; 239m Ralph A. Clevenger/ CORBIS; 241ml Chinch Gryniewicz, Ecoscene/CORBIS; 241r Hans Strand/ CORBIS; 242mr Randy Wells/CORBIS
Courtesy Luca Pietranera, Telespazio, Rome, Italy: 228ml
Courtesy Michael P. Frankis: 222bm
Digital Vision: 202bl; 203; 205tr, br; 214l; 224br; 227b; 228bl; 229tl, r; 239b; 242ml, b; 243tr, ml, br; 244bl, br; 245ml, b
Dr Ben Wigham/Ian Hudson, Southampton Oceanography Centre: 234bl
Getty Images: Cover Getty Images/Georgette Douwma; 194-195 Getty Images/Richard Price; 223br Getty Images/Darrell Gulin; 228br Getty Images/Pete Turner; 229bm Getty Images/William J. Hebert; 232 Getty Images/Erik Leigh Simmons; 238mr Getty Images/Photodisc, 238b Getty Images/Paul Souders; 243bl Getty Images/Antonio M. Rosario
Science Photo Library: Cover Scott Camazine/Science Photo Library; 208bl Peter Menzel/Science Photo Library, 208br Mark A. Schneider/Science Photo Library; 235br Dr Ken Macdonald/Science Photo Library
Historic Royal Palaces: 210bl Crown copyright: Historic Royal Palaces. Reproduced by permission of Historic Royal Palaces under licence from the controller of Her Majesty's Stationery Office
James A. Pisarowicz PhD: 218mr
NASA/Goddard Spaceflight Center Scientific Visualization Studio: 237m
National Aeronautics and Space Administration (NASA): 246t
National Oceanic and Atmospheric Administration (NOAA)/Dept of Commerce: 237b
Natural History Picture Agency (NHPA): 218bl NHPA/Stephen Krasemann
Photograph by the late R.K. Pilsbury, Royal MeteorologicalSociety: 204l
Richard D. Fisher: 219
Robert M. Reed: 208tr
U.S. Department of Interior, United States Geological Survey (USGS): 214r, 215tm, tr
US Navy: 236bl
USGS: 205mr USGS/Cascades Volcano Observatory, photographer: M. P. Doukas
www.patagonia.com: 244tr

Illustrators Jerry Gower, Ian Jackson, Malcolm McGregor, Annabel Milne, Tricia Newell, Michelle Ross, Peter Stebbing, David Wright
Additional design Joanne Kirkby, Laura Hammonds, Candice Whatmore
Additional editing Sarah Khan, Elizabeth Dalby
Managing designers Ruth Russell, Karen Tomlins
Series editor Judy Tatchell

Usborne Publishing is not responsible and does not accept liability for the availability or content of any website other than its own, or for any exposure to harmful, offensive, or inaccurate material which may appear on the Web. Usborne Publishing will have no liability for any damage or loss caused by viruses that may be downloaded as a result of browsing the sites it recommends.

Material in this book is based on *The Usborne Book of Animal Facts and Lists* by Anita Ganeri © Usborne Publishing, 1988; *The Usborne Book of Ocean Facts and Lists* by Anita Ganeri © Usborne Publishing, 1990; *The Usborne Book of Prehistoric Facts and Lists* by Annabel Craig, © Usborne Publishing, 1986; *The Usborne Book of Earth Facts and Lists* by Lynn Bresler, © Usborne Publishing, 1986.